Frankfort

SAVING

GREENING THE BLUEGRASS

KENTUCKY

A PORTION OF THE PROCEEDS FROM

THIS BOOK WILL SUPPORT THE WORK OF

KENTUCKIANS FOR THE COMMONWEALTH

TO HELP SAVE THE MOUNTAINS AND

HERITAGE OF EASTERN KENTUCKY FROM

MOUNTAINTOP REMOVAL AND VALLEY FILLS.

COPYRIGHT © 2010

LIMESTONE LANE PRESS

423 SWING LANE LOUISVILLE, KY 40207
SavingKentucky.com

PRODUCED BY CRESCENT HILL BOOKS
CrescentHillBooks.com

ISBN 978-0-9674208-1-3

*Printed by Everbest Printing Co. LTD, Nansha, China
5-11-2010
87395.3*

IN MEMORY OF

SCOTT TICHENOR,

WHO TAUGHT US

ABOUT SAVING THE

IMPORTANT

THINGS.

F O

F {

W O

We are born of the land and buried in the earth. People are a product not only of their family heritage but also of their surroundings and the food they eat. These factors shape us as we grow and in turn leave our mark on the world.

Saving Kentucky is about two things: Kentucky's land—our "common wealth"—and our people. Our valuable land is slowly eroding because of several factors, among them the desire for cheap energy; the corporate greed that externalizes the true cost of mountaintop-removal coal mining; unsustainable development and urban sprawl; and perhaps a misguided definition of progress, where anything new is considered better.

As we move deeper into the twenty-first century, our past—vanishing though it may be—becomes ever more important. While this book heralds in some ways a bygone era that can never truly be reclaimed in an age of rapid communication and Tweets, I take comfort in knowing that there are folks who

R E
R D

treasure and cherish this past. A study of the past and our heritage helps us feel part of the larger human race and part of a cultural history that has defined us.

This ambitious project catalogs some of the heroes and unique places of Kentucky and challenges us to think about what deserves preserving in our own neighborhoods. Many places in America have lost any sense of identity. Strip malls in one town are the same as in any other town. It pains me to think that aliens dropped down in most American towns would see no immediate local identifying marks.

So this is a book about valuable places and significant people. Enjoy, and leave it on your fair-trade coffee table for others to enjoy. Make a commitment to spend your hard-earned dollars locally. Support the folks in this book, and continue to nurture the land of Kentucky.

GILL HOLLAND

Gill is an award-winning independent film and music producer and noted preservationist in the "NuLu" East Market District of Louisville, Kentucky. In 2007, with wife, Augusta, he developed The Green Building, an innovative renovation that heralds a new era of sustainable urban design for Kentucky.

I Owe So Much To So Many

| Henlee Barnette |

I have been fed from fields

I did not till.

I have crossed bridges

I did not build.

I have sat in the shade of trees

I did not plant.

I have received knowledge

I did not research.

I have been guided by lights

I did not turn on.

TABLE OF

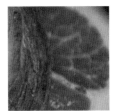

CONTENTS

INTRODUCTION

SAVING KENTUCKY

SAVING KENTUCKY IS ABOUT
SAVING NOT ONLY LANDSCAPE AND
HISTORIC PROPERTY BUT ALSO
A WAY OF LIFE. IT TELLS THE
STORIES, IN PICTURES AND WORDS,
OF AN ECLECTIC GROUP OF
KENTUCKIANS WHO ARE CHANGING
THEIR STATE'S FUTURE BY
PRESERVING ITS PAST.
THEY ARE UNIQUE INDIVIDUALS,
FROM THE POETIC TO THE VISIONARY,
FROM THE GUTSY TO THE GRACEFUL,
WHO ARE DEEPLY CONNECTED TO
THEIR HERITAGE AND ARE DOING
EXTRAORDINARY THINGS TO USHER
THE OLD WAYS INTO A NEW ERA.

A NATIONAL CHAMPION
BUR OAK AT AIRDRIE

Saving Kentucky sprang from my admiration for an interior designer from Louisville, Scott Tichenor, who taught me about saving the important things. Scott taught me not only to cherish family belongings but to find a place for them and share their memories so that the pieces would have meaning and history— so that they would tell a story. It is important to learn about your roots, he said, because if you are comfortable with who you are, your life will be easier. Scott taught me that in a like way, saving old buildings and old land adds immeasurably to the soul of a place. My friend had thought a lot about these things, and he passed his interest along to me.

Saving Kentucky is about saving not only landscape and historic property but also a way of life. It tells the stories, in pictures and words, of an eclectic group of Kentuckians who are changing their state's future by preserving its past. They are unique individuals, from the poetic to the visionary, from the gutsy to the graceful, who are deeply connected to their heritage and are doing extraordinary things to usher the old ways into a new era. Their stories range in vision, and although some have the resources to match that vision, many are people of average means but singular determination.

You will meet Jimmy Middleton, a country doctor and farmer who understands the economics of bringing the land back to the way it was three hundred years ago. His efforts to plant thousands of trees and acres of native grasses on his land along the Green River will, he knows, protect the river from erosion and wash-off chemicals and improve its environment. "The Green River is special," he says. "According to the Nature Conservancy, it's one of North America's most diverse ecosystems."

You will meet the Carloftis family, who live in the foothills of the Cumberland Mountains and whose youngest son, Jon, took his Kentucky roots to the rooftop gardens of New York City, where he speaks nature to his clients. Those roots trace back to the family's Fort Sequoyah Indian Village, a tourist stop on Highway 25, the story of which is, in a word, fabulous.

You will meet Kathy Cary, chef-owner of Lilly's in Louisville, which features local farm products on the menu and is known as one of the finest restaurants in the southeast. Kathy, a pioneer in the effort to help Kentucky farmers get healthy, fresh food to the people, grew up on her parents' three-hundred-acre farm. There she developed a oneness with nature which, together with her delight in discovering that she could create divine meals from her mother's garden, set the stage for a restaurant of her own.

Chuck Smith and Mary Berry Smith are eighth-generation farmers in Henry County. Less than ten years ago they were traditional Kentucky farmers growing mainly tobacco and raising dairy cattle. "But we could see the handwriting on the wall," says Mary. "It had been evident for a while that tobacco would not survive, and we had begun to think about things we could do that would let us continue to farm—and have something to leave our children if they chose to stay." Today the family-operated Smith-Berry Winery raises three kinds of grapes and makes nineteen kinds of wine.

Mary's father, the writer Wendell Berry, has said that "small farms and small communities are as vital to our liberties now as they were in Jefferson's day." I spoke with Wendell and his wife, Tanya, one chilly Sunday afternoon in the warm kitchen of their Henry County farmhouse. These wonderful people, brilliant and warm, made me comfortable immediately. Wendell talked about what Kentucky had been through as an agrarian state, and about his hopes for the future. He talked about tobacco, from the great art of growing it to the effect that its demise had on farmers. His voice and those of other beloved Kentuckians resonate throughout *Saving Kentucky*.

I began to absorb the idea of preservation at an early age—in spite of myself. I don't remember being particularly interested in history, or in historic preservation, as a young person growing up in Kentucky, but I do remember the night in the late fifties when my father asked if I would like to go with him to visit a lady named Mrs. Waters who lived on the hill one over from ours. It was dark as we parked the car at the end of the gravel driveway and crunched through the unkempt yard toward a big, dark house. We went through the door into the kitchen. It was hard to see in the dim light of the oil lamp, and I remember linoleum coming up from the floor and wallpaper peeling off the walls. I followed my father up the stairs to the bedside of a very, very old lady. Mrs. Waters had long white hair, long fingernails, and a raspy voice.

Now, just about everyone liked my father. He was warm and easy to like, and I guess Mrs. Waters did, too. Why else would she allow him to visit her like this—an old woman in a long white gown, on what was probably her deathbed? He sat beside her and they talked for a few minutes—about the house and her family. I don't remember what was said, but I like to think that he was telling her how her home was going to be someday, and how it would be loved and visited by many people.

Locust Grove was one of the first fine brick homes built in the Kentucky district of Virginia, and according to Louisville historian Dr. Sam Thomas, it is probably the earliest brick house still standing in Kentucky. It was built in 1790 by William and Lucy Croghan, who lived there along with, in later years, Lucy's brother, the famous General George Rogers Clark, founder of Louisville. My father was the second Regent of Locust Grove, and the historic home opened on his watch. I like to think that Mrs. Waters would be well pleased. So I do remember that historic preservation was important around our house, but we were a distilling family, and my parents mostly had their hands full with that. Our family made bourbon. The Stitzel-Weller Distillery was started by my grandfather, and for a large part of the twentieth century it was known for making the finest bourbon in the world. It was sold in 1972. That sense of loss caused me—twenty years later—to write *But Always Fine Bourbon*.

The same impulse that drove me to write *But Always Fine Bourbon* has inspired *Saving Kentucky*. Too often we don't know what we have until we lose it. So in the past few years, I have traveled Kentucky, hiking through the Cumberland Gap, driving up and down two-lane roads where sagging tobacco barns bear witness to an industry so important but now all but gone from the landscape. I have stopped in towns so tiny as to be one or two blocks long—where the people are close. I have traveled the roads of the Bluegrass—mile after mile of low stone walls snaking through the Thoroughbred horse farms that are legendary to the state. I have seen first-hand both the majesty and the heartbreak of the eastern Appalachian Mountains and the people who live in them—and it has been a privilege.

As we watch this flat world changing with lightning speed, we are seeing the disappearance of much that has given this country its rich sense of place. Because of its fertile soil, Kentucky has long teemed with farms, large and small, especially in the central part of the state. That farming way of life hung on here far longer than in other states—twenty to thirty years longer—because of tobacco. It is because of tobacco and the small family farms that grew it that so much luscious land is left. But today, the hard fact is that development is more profitable than agricultural use, and Kentucky loses 130 acres of agricultural land—per day—to development.

In eastern Kentucky, coal companies practice mountaintop strip mining, blasting off the tops of the oldest mountains in the world and pushing the rubble into the valleys, burying streams that used to be clear and shining, or clogging them with noxious waste. The people who live in these mountains are our people, and this land is part of our heritage.

All over this country, Main Street and even whole towns are being lost—closed down and forgotten. Main Street was an institution. Where has it gone? Scott Tichenor would point out, "People used to sit on their front porch and wave and talk to people going by. Today they don't know their neighbors. They close their doors and turn on their air-conditioning and watch TV."

Because of these situations and many more, the consciousness of our nation is undergoing a major shift, and change has become a buzzword. People seem to feel they have lost something. Maybe they have lost their way because they have lost their past. "When we are surrounded by things that are meaningful to us," Scott used to say, "we begin to feel connected to our surroundings, connected to one another and to ourselves. Then life becomes full and deep."

In his book *Last Child in the Woods*, Richard Louv talks about the fact that children don't play in creeks and roam in woods anymore. Eventually, he says, that's going to have a huge impact on society. Research shows that connections and experiences with the natural environment are critical to our physical, mental, moral, and spiritual development. The people in *Saving Kentucky* are a living testament to the value of such ties and the miracles they inspire.

The heritage that Kathy Cary, the Carloftis family, Jimmy Middleton, and others are at pains to preserve is not just theirs—belonging, that is, to a few people in a few pockets of rural Kentucky—but ours, and that of our children and grandchildren. True to our country's pioneering ancestry, their stories chronicle a humble but heroic valor in facing the challenges of the twenty-first century, and we hope that they will inspire you to do something as well—to save the place that is your home.

LOCUST GROVE

BECAUSE OF THESE SITUATIONS AND MANY MORE, THE CONSCIOUSNESS OF OUR NATION IS UNDERGOING A MAJOR SHIFT, AND CHANGE HAS BECOME A BUZZWORD. PEOPLE SEEM TO FEEL THEY HAVE LOST SOMETHING. MAYBE THEY HAVE LOST THEIR WAY BECAUSE THEY HAVE LOST THEIR PAST. "WHEN WE ARE SURROUNDED BY THINGS THAT ARE MEANINGFUL TO US," SCOTT USED TO SAY, "WE BEGIN TO FEEL CONNECTED TO OUR SURROUNDINGS, CONNECTED TO ONE ANOTHER AND TO OURSELVES. THEN LIFE BECOMES FULL AND DEEP."

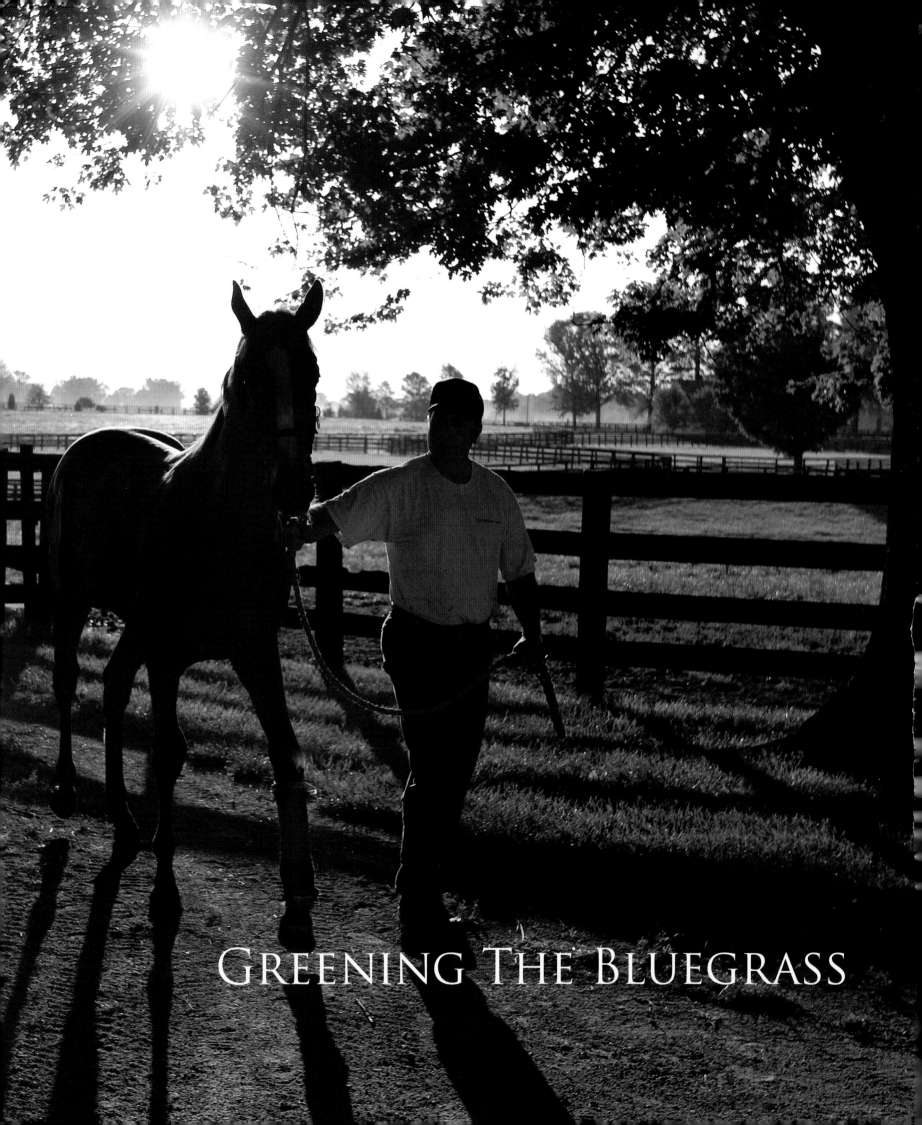

GREENING THE BLUEGRASS

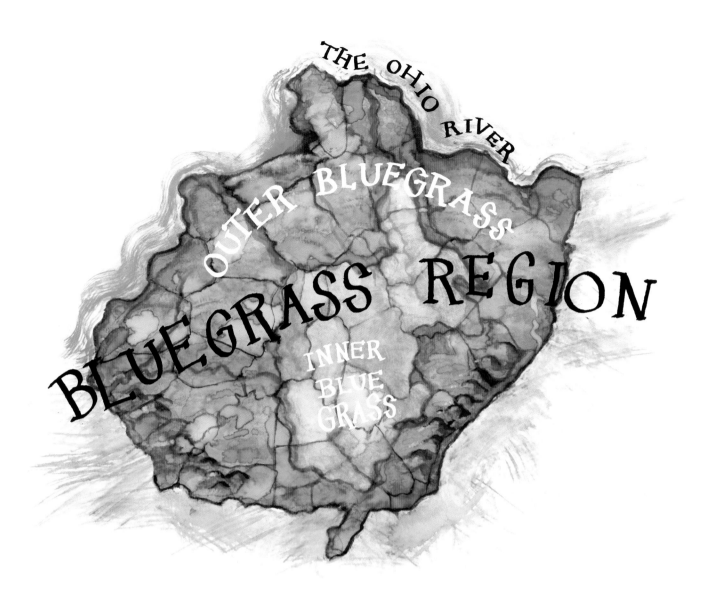

THE OHIO RIVER

OUTER BLUEGRASS

BLUEGRASS REGION

INNER BLUE GRASS

Of the major regions of Kentucky, the best known by far sits smack in the middle of the state: the Bluegrass. The name conjures up images of rich, rolling farmland, shady lanes, low rock walls, plank fencing and, of course, Thoroughbreds.

It is estimated that Kentucky-bred horses account for 82 percent of the total value of horses sold in the United States. That includes horses for fox hunting, eventing, polo, trail riding, pony riding, and just plain old horseback riding. There are standardbreds, quarter horses, Kentucky Mountain Saddle Horses, Arabians, and the list goes on. But what everyone knows best is that Kentucky's Bluegrass is the place where the breeding and racing of Thoroughbreds is king. Farms with names like Calumet and Claiborne, Lane's End and Gainesborough, Airdrie, Ashford, and Three Chimneys are known internationally, and Queen Elizabeth II boards many of her brood mares at Lane's End.

Why here? What makes the Bluegrass so special? The answer lies in the soil.

More than 450 million years ago, when the eastern part of the continent was still under water, great collisions on the earth's surface caused the Appalachian Mountains to form, arching the earth's crust to the west. One of these arches formed a high plateau measuring fifty miles wide and several hundred miles long, reaching from what is now Ohio through central Kentucky to southern Tennessee. This huge area of high ground consists largely of limestone covered in dark brown soil that is unusually rich in phosphate. The grass that grows from this soil is uniquely able to nurture strong bones in animals that graze on it. And the greatest concentration of the soil is in the Fayette County area, the heart of the Bluegrass.

The Outer Bluegrass is bordered by the Ohio River in the north and west and a ring of hills known as the Knobs in the west, south, and east. It encompasses the city of Louisville, home of the Kentucky Derby. That legendary race, run at Churchill Downs on the first Saturday in May, draws celebrities and dignitaries from all over the world, and anyone without a lump in his throat at the first strains of "My Old Kentucky Home" must be from another planet. As Kentucky humorist Irwin S. Cobb put it, "Until you go to Kentucky and with your own eyes behold a Derby, you ain't been nowhere and you ain't seen nothing."

The more fertile Inner Bluegrass includes some of the most prosperous farmland in the state. Its hub is Lexington, where Keeneland draws the equine aristocracy with its spring and fall meets as well as its September sale of some of the most valuable horses in the world. It is this region of rolling grassland nourished by limestone-rich soils that has made Kentucky the horse capital of the world.

Drive down the old turnpikes and rural roads that fan out from Lexington, through pastureland rife with romping foals, past open-sided tobacco barns, down the Main Streets of tiny Midway and Versailles. This is a gentle land where life moves at a leisurely pace. The people here are innately and of necessity close to the land, and there is an earthiness about them that is both disarming and charming.

Thomas Clark, Kentucky's beloved historian laureate, probably summed it up best when he said, "The Bluegrass is not only a region that can be defined on a map. It is a state of mind, a way of life."

And yet, in 2006, the World Monuments Fund named Kentucky's Bluegrass region one of the most endangered places on the planet.

Thomas Clark, Kentucky's beloved historian laureate,
probably summed it up best when he said,
"The Bluegrass is not only a region that can be defined
on a map. It is a state of mind, a way of life."

And yet, in 2006, the World Monuments Fund named Kentucky's
Bluegrass region one of the most endangered
places on the planet.

A NATIONAL CHAMPION
BUR OAK AT AIRDRIE

Land
Of Milk
And Honey

Libby Jones knows the Bluegrass intimately. She has fought for it. It's in her blood. As she speaks of it the words roll off her tongue with urgency, as they often do with people whose heart and soul are poured into a thing.

I went to see the Joneses one hot afternoon at the height of a summer drought, and while this busy couple had plenty of things to tend to, they made me feel as if my project was theirs as well. We sat on the screened porch and talked of the two things that, next to family, are most important to them: the Thoroughbred industry and the land.

"The Bluegrass was the first settlement," Libby said. "When Daniel Boone and his family came through the Cumberland Gap and made their way into the Inner Bluegrass, they had come a long way—through mountains, through terrain that was wooded and steep-sloped. These were people who needed to make their living off the land. They came to the Bluegrass because it was the land of milk and honey. It had the finest soil; it was arable land; it was reasonably flat."

The region "was so precious in its capacity for production and so rich in water and soil resources that the Indians—the Native Kentuckians—recognized it to be a rare and remarkable place. One of their names for this place that was to become Kentucky was Land of Tomorrow. They considered it a Garden of Eden.

Bluegrass

{ | LIBBY & BRERETON JONES | | AIRDRIE |

| WOODBURN |

1

"Those early white settlers made this their home, and since then, I think our reputation internationally for raising the finest of pedigreed animals is possible because of the quality and composition of the soil.

OLD FRANKFORT PIKE
Photo courtesy of The Kentucky Historical Society

"Brerry and I have many foreign visitors from all over the globe, and they have a deep appreciation for this land. There's something so inherently beautiful and yet even fragile about it. I feel a sense of vulnerability in this landscape, because you know that it could be destroyed so easily."

As a student at Manhattan's Finch College back in the sixties, Libby often crunched numbers far into the night, balancing the books of her family farm in Woodford County. Airdrie, where she grew up, sits across the Old Frankfort Pike from Woodburn, established in the nineteenth century by her great-great uncle, Robert A. Alexander. Under him, Woodburn became the birthplace of Kentucky's modern Thoroughbred industry.

THE JONESES MOVED TO WOODFORD COUNTY AT A
TIME THAT WAS TO PROVE CRUCIAL IN THE REGION'S HISTORY.
CHANGE WAS COMING.

The son of a West Virginia dairy farmer and successful entrepreneur, Brereton Jones grew up reading books like Black Beauty, My Friend Flicka, and Misty of Chincoteague. "I was taken with horses," he says. "Always." He and Libby married in 1970 and lived for a time in Huntington, West Virginia, where Brereton began raising a few modest Thoroughbreds. But Libby longed for Kentucky. "I began to realize how much she genuinely loved that land," says Brereton. In 1972, the Joneses arranged with Libby's father to lease part of Airdrie. Together, over time, they converted Airdrie from a farm raising cattle, tobacco, and row crops to a Thoroughbred breeding farm.

The Joneses moved to Woodford County at a time that was to prove crucial in the region's history. Change was coming.

"In 1972," Libby explains, "this area was a quiet and very peaceful agrarian community with one hundred percent devotion to raising crops and animals. Then, an investor from Chicago saw a development opportunity in a farm next door to our farm." As described by Ben Chandler, editor of *The Woodford Sun*, Charter Oaks was to be a classic example of a leapfrog development: a 725-acre subdivision with 125 homes on five-acre lots with no sewers and a rural water and fire district on a two-lane road—a beautifully designed development but in the wrong place. It would be, he said, "as if it were dropped down into the most achingly beautiful, prime farmland of the entire county—and maybe of the world."

The Charter Oaks subdivision was an immediate call to arms. "Those of us who lived in this area were horrified at the prospect," Libby says, "because we saw, long-range that this was just the beginning. If this farm fell to development, it would be the old domino theory, and pretty soon this whole area would wind up being houses instead of farms.

"There was a meeting of those most immediately affected, and to the last man, woman, and child we decided to fight. And that's how Woodford Save the Land was started. We incorporated. We went to Planning and Zoning. Everyone said, 'You can't fight City Hall. It's progress. It's a done deal.' But we said no, this land is too precious to Woodford County and to the whole world as

Bluegrass land, and we fought it. It took time, and it took money, and it took a tremendous amount of work, but we won. In the end, the planning and zoning commissioners changed their minds and voted against it. And at that point we recognized that we did have a voice and we could make things happen. So that was the beginning, and today the word is out that any project that will convert farmland to other uses in this county will be analyzed not just by the people in the Courthouse but by a broad-based citizen band. They are going to look at that project and analyze whether they think it's a benefit or a detriment to this county as a whole. And if they think it's a detriment, you can be sure that they are going to be at every public hearing, and they are going to lobby their public officials, and there is going to be a whale of a fight."

beautiful and innovative horse barns in Kentucky and became so respected as a horseman that he was dubbed "the Wizard of the Turf."

Today, Hamburg Place is a gargantuan development, a huge retail complex with big box stores spilling into what were once pristine pastures. Thousands of houses have either been built or are in the planning stage, and the training barns, which John Madden designed so that two horses could be ridden side by side (the stalls were fitted with oak kick plates twenty-four inches wide), have come down. The developer is John Madden's great-grandson, Patrick Madden, whose family still owns the property. "It became impractical to farm it as a horse farm," he says, "with the Interstate, three sewers, two water lines, and an electric station running through the place.

> 66 Today, instead of the proposed 725-acre Charter Oaks subdivision, the land along US 60 is the site of the gloriously green Gainsborough Farm. 'And if you compare growth here with that in surrounding counties, Woodford County is like an oasis.' 99
> —Libby Jones

According to the World Monuments Fund, by 2007 the Inner Bluegrass had lost to development more than 80,000 of its 1.2 million acres, mostly around Lexington, where the population has more than doubled in recent years. That expansion has put tremendous development pressure on the ten surrounding counties that, together with Fayette, make up the Inner Bluegrass. With less and less land available to build on within the urban service area of Fayette County, the rural landscape has sprouted subdivisions and strip malls, and the price of land has skyrocketed.

The most poignant example of this is probably the famed Hamburg Place, the ravishing two thousand–acre horse farm on the northern outskirts of Lexington, which produced seven Kentucky Derby winners. John E. Madden, who bought the property in 1898, designed and built some of the most

When the city grew up against it, it became silly from an economic standpoint to raise horses on it."

In 1999, the city raised the minimum lot size in rural Fayette County from ten acres to forty, and in 2000, the county approved a conservation easement program, one of the best tools in existence for preserving land. Since then, growth in Fayette County has been largely contained to the core of Lexington, but by the time the measures were adopted a lot of ground— literally—had been lost.

Fayette's conservation easement program allows the county to purchase development rights from a property owner for an amount determined by two certified appraisals.

 I THINK COUNTIES ALL OVER KENTUCKY ARE RECOGNIZING HOW VITAL IT IS TO TAKE AN ACTIVIST ROLE IN PROTECTING FARMLAND ... AND WE'RE NOT ALONE. WE SHARE THAT CHALLENGE WITH ALL BEAUTIFUL PLACES IN THE WORLD.

—Libby Jones

The first appraisal determines the fair market value of the land if it were to be sold for development; the second determines what the same land would sell for as a farm. The difference in the two appraisals is the value of the conservation easement and the amount the owner receives. He can keep his land as a farm, sell it as a farm, or will it to an heir, but that land can never be developed.

Woodford County adopted a similar program in 2009, but without funding. The hope is that funds will be found—and that the USDA might match those funds. Elsewhere, farms can donate their conservation easements in exchange for a tax credit—though this is not a viable option for the many farmers who barely eke out a living. In the Inner Bluegrass, these easements are held by the Bluegrass Conservancy, a private 501(c)(3).

PACE—Purchase of Agricultural Conservation Easements—is a nationally recognized conservation program that has been used for some time by states such as New York, Maryland, and Pennsylvania. When Brereton Jones was elected governor in 1991, Libby saw a chance to promote conservation easements at the state level. In 1994, thanks in large part to her efforts, Kentucky became the first Southern state to adopt the program. Long known as a strong advocate for the family farm, Brereton Jones wishes he had done more. "In retrospect," says the former governor, "I should have called a special legislative session relative to the PACE program so that we would have had some permanent funding, but that didn't happen. The hope is that down the road it will." It's been a tough political sale in Kentucky, however: money for "wealthy horse people" when there's so much poverty in the state.

"I think counties all over Kentucky are recognizing how vital it is for their quality of life and for their economy to take an activist role in protecting farmland," says Libby, "because if we don't do that, we are going to soon lose the balance between what we've always been known for and what we do best—which is agriculture—to urbanization. Just plain sprawl. And we're not alone. We share that challenge with all beautiful places in the world."

The equine industry is one of Kentucky's leading agricultural generators and a main catalyst for tourism, with an estimated $4 billion impact on the state's economy each year. "We all know that if the land is desecrated, everybody's in trouble," says Brereton, "from feed farmers, to blacksmiths, to veterinarians, to farm workers, and everyone in between.

"You cannot save Kentucky as we know it and love it if you don't save the horse industry, because this land will end up under concrete. With that understood, you have to find a way for horses to thrive and compete. It's got to be a viable business."

In 2004, Brereton Jones and the late John Gaines started the Kentucky Equine Education Project, or KEEP. "I was concerned that there was no unification of the horse industry. Everyone was pulling in different directions, and there was no group that coordinated all of the horse interests. And not just Thoroughbreds but standardbred, walking horses, show horses. There are as many quarter horses in Kentucky as there are Thoroughbreds, if not more." KEEP works to let Kentuckians know how important the horse industry is to the economic well-being of the state so they'll be more inclined to help preserve it.

The former governor, like so many others, thinks that bringing casino gambling to the racetracks where gambling already exists is the only way to go. Kentucky racetracks and horsemen have complained for years that larger purses in states with expanded gambling revenues are hurting the industry here. They believe it is both fair and logical for Kentucky's horse industry to be allowed to compete on a level playing field with the competition. A little over a decade ago, a Las Vegas company built a $300 million casino in rural Harrison County, Indiana, just downstream from Louisville. "That facility and others like it in Southern Indiana put significant pressure on Churchill Downs and the entire horse racing industry in the state of Kentucky," says John Asher, Churchill Downs' vice president for racing communications. That pressure has intensified, and today the grim reality is that more and more horsemen are pulling up stakes and leaving Kentucky for more favorable economic climates.

"What has to happen for the industry to survive," says Brereton, "is that people have to feel that they have at least a reasonable chance of not losing too much money when they put a horse in training. We know that the odds of winning the Kentucky Derby are astronomical, but if you have a reasonable chance of breaking even, or making a little profit, or even of not losing too much, and having a lot of fun doing it, that's the way I think the Thoroughbred industry needs to be perceived.

"So that's the reason we've got to get the purses up, and the way you do that is to let the gambling come to the tracks and then designate that a percent of that money goes into the purse structure—a percentage of it goes into education, a percentage of it goes into health care, et cetera."

There is no farm in all of the Bluegrass that holds more history than Woodburn. Woodburn was a land grant, originally, the property of General Hugh Mercer, to whom it had been granted for military service during the Revolutionary War. In 1790, after Mercer's death, a Scotsman by the name of Robert Alexander bought the Mercer estate. It was his son, R. A. Alexander, Libby Jones's great-great-uncle, who established the farm that became the birthplace of Kentucky's Thoroughbred industry, the first commercial breeding operation in the United States. Educated at Cambridge, R. A. Alexander imported only the best livestock from Europe—equine, bovine, swine, and sheep.

WOODBURN
Now under protection of
a conservation easement

He began the first American Stud Book and created what is now the American Jockey Club. Until that time, people traded horses or sold them privately. R. A. Alexander was the first to have a public auction for yearlings, the forerunner of the Keeneland and Fasig Tipton sales.

"People would come all the way from New York on the train to Spring Station, Kentucky," says Libby, "and get into a horse-drawn carriage and come over here to a woodland savannah at Woodburn. That's where they would have the auction. Today the process of preparing a yearling for sale is exhaustive. Back then they just hauled that baby up to that location and sold him under the trees."

"When Woodburn came on the market," Brereton recalls, "Libby came to me in true distress. I said, 'Libby, we are land-poor now. We cannot afford to buy any more land.' " But as weeks passed, Brereton would drive down the road past Woodburn, and "it began to dawn on me what could happen to that farm—how sick we all would be."

In 2002, the Joneses purchased the 495-acre Woodburn property (which had by that time become a cattle farm again) and placed the entire farm under a conservation easement, ensuring that it would never be developed. They then began to restore the property. "The house," says Brereton, "needed a dramatic amount of work. People asked if we were going to tear it down. But of course, it's so special. Four Derby winners were raised here, nine Preakness winners, ten Belmont winners. Now we've gotten it so we can raise horses on it again."

Proud Spell, one of the first to be raised at Woodburn, was a late foal. "She was quite small," Brereton remembers, "and we felt that if we took her to the sale she wouldn't bring much money, if any." They decided to race her.

"We broke her right after the sale and turned her out for the winter," says Brereton. "She'd spend twenty-three hours a day out in the snow, the wind, the rain. A lot of Thoroughbreds are hot-housed and pampered, and quite frankly, historically I think it's pretty easy to prove that you don't raise as good a horse that way."

As a two-year-old, Proud Spell won lots of races—and $600,000—against some of the best fillies in the world. "Then we'd bring her back to the farm, turn her out, let her eat some good grass, get some good Kentucky sunshine. In late December, we sent her to New Orleans, then to Keeneland, and then on to the Kentucky Oaks."

On the third of May 2008, Proud Spell won the Kentucky Oaks by five lengths. Her sire, Proud Citizen, stands stud at Airdrie.

Today, Libby continues to support such preservation efforts as the Bluegrass Conservancy, the Woodford Coalition, and the PACE program. She also sits on the board of the American Farmland Trust and remains optimistic about the future.

"I THINK WE HAVE BEEN VERY BLESSED THAT PEOPLE HERE ARE WILLING TO PUT THEIR TIME AND TALENT AND TREASURE ON THE LINE BECAUSE THEY CARE SO IMMENSELY ABOUT THIS PLACE. BECAUSE WHEN IT'S GONE, IT'S GONE. ONCE YOU COVER LAND WITH CONCRETE, IT'S GONE FOREVER."

—Libby Jones

Around Central Kentucky, there is no one more able to provide perspective on the sport of kings than Robert E. Courtney, who bought his first broodmare, Sweet Face, in 1941 for fifty dollars and retired sixty-seven years later at the age of eighty-six. On the January afternoon that he sold his last mare, the Keeneland sale was silenced to recognize the man.

I was privileged to spend a morning with Mr. Courtney at his beloved Crestfield Farm outside Lexington while he gave me his view of the Thoroughbred industry and how it has evolved over the past seventy years. The industry has been in a chaotic state of late, with the horrific breakdowns of first Barbaro and then Eight Bells before millions of fans nationwide. Those events resulted in widespread calls to make the sport safer. The shock waves reached all the way to Washington, prompting a congressional hearing that raised complicated issues, from drugs, to track surfaces, to breeding practices.

"Years ago, people around here didn't raise horses as a business," Mr. Courtney told me. "They were all farmers. They raised cattle, sheep, hogs, and everything else, and they raised horses on the side. It was just a product of their farm, that's what it was. But today, it's big business.

"Back in the thirties we had a little gentlemen's trotting club—called it the Red Mile. They'd meet out there every other Saturday. These were all farmers that trained their own horses. They'd have a little race meeting, and if anybody fouled anybody then they'd

have a steward's inquiry. And the fine was always a quart of whiskey. Well, when the meet was over you'd congregate on the backside and have a little drink. Drank up the foul, you know. So 'course somebody was always going to get fouled—you knew that.

"After World War II the tax laws changed. The economy grew in this country, and the horse business grew with it. Wealthy people wanted to get involved because of tax advantages—well, that and the glory of having a good horse. The Whitneys and the Wideners moved in and established their farms up the Paris Pike—that was the Wall Street of the horse business for a while—and there was Colonel Bradley on the Old Frankfort Pike and John Geppert over at Idle Hour. That raised the ante a little bit, and everybody got more horses involved. The industry grew and grew, and by the late forties, early fifties, big farms got to where they were raising nothing but horses. So the whole thing started as a farm issue— and now it was a business issue," he says, with a big emphasis on the word *business*.

Sometimes, when a talented three-year-old wins one or more of the major stakes races, he will be pulled from the racetrack,

assigned to the stud barn, and syndicated for a lot of money. So a brilliant horse that has become a hero—with potential for drawing thousands of fans, time after time, to the track—will be seen no more. And the stud fee for that horse could be upwards of $100,000—beyond the means of many small farms. Mr. Courtney has stayed in business, he says, by having a good partner and by sticking to his philosophy of breeding to "proven" stallions—solid sires in the middle of the market that provide value.

"Those big outfits have got to get the money out of a stallion in the first two years he's standing at stud, because if he doesn't get that good runner in that first crop of foals, his value goes down. So they set the stud fee up, and you're going in and buying these untried horses. But you've paid a lot of money when you breed to one of these stallions, and you're taking a big chance. You've got to take what God gives you when a horse gets born.

Not all of them are perfect, and damn few are—let's be frank about it. So I make it a practice to breed to stallions that are older and already established, because I know these horses sire horses that can race."

Mr. Courtney's track record and his survival in a business that can make paupers of millionaires speak to his skill and wisdom. His most successful purchase was the mare Hasty Queen II: "I bought her for eleven thousand dollars and sold about a million dollars' worth of yearlings out of her."

The man has a world of friends and admirers. He has dispensed advice and knowledge to dozens of people starting out in the horse business, and he's been there to guide them through the inevitable rocky times. He is also a realist. "I worry about the future," he says. "How the little man is going exist, I don't know."

Crestfield Farm is now for sale, but Mr. Courtney still owns a few mares in partnership with his son Robert Jr., who is carrying on the family trade. "I'm not going get completely out of the horse business," Mr. C says definitively. "This is a disease."

So does he have any advice for surviving in the business if you're just starting out, or if you are a small breeder?

"Pray," Mr. Courtney answers with a twinkle. "And you have to be lucky, too."

WELCOME HALL

TWO
CENTURIES
& SEVEN
GENERATIONS

Welcome Hall sits well off the Clifton Road at the end of a long entrance in Woodford County. It is listed on the National Register of Historic Places and is one of the oldest homes in the state. Because the old farm has changed little over the years, it provides an unusually clear window to the past. The Graddys didn't like change.

On a warm spring day, Kitty Graddy Tonkin, the fiery 84-year-old matriarch of the Graddy family and the current mistress of Welcome Hall, sits on a wicker sofa on the back veranda, her foot resting on the coffee table, her back against the cool stone wall. Widowed in 1985, Kitty lives here with her second husband, William Tonkin. "The Graddys have farmed this land for a long time," she says, looking past the icehouse to acres of fertile fields, "and I think there's something about farming that gives your life more meaning than anything else. Sure, you have to have development, but not at the expense of something as unique as this land.

"If we can take care of it, two hundred years from now it will still be beautiful and productive. If we plant houses on it, it'll be gone forever."

Determination

| WELCOME HALL |

{ | THE GRADDY FAMILY | 2

THE DEVELOPERS WANTED TO TAKE MORE AND MORE OF THIS FABULOUS FARMLAND THAT WE HAVE HERE AND TURN IT INTO SUBDIVISIONS, AND IT MADE ME SO MAD THAT I HAD 5,000 BUMPER STICKERS MADE UP THAT SAID 'GROWTH DESTROYS BLUEGRASS—FOREVER.'

—Kitty Graddy Tonkin

Ten years ago a group of developers took out a full-page ad in the Lexington Herald-Leader that read, "Growth is good—let's make Lexington grow better" and made a case for development in this corner of the Bluegrass. Having crossed the Rubicon, they came face to face with Kitty Tonkin. "They said that it made your taxes lower," Kitty recalls, "which was not so. They said that there was plenty of land left to develop, which was not so. The developers wanted to take more and more of this fabulous farmland that we have here and turn it into subdivisions, and it made me so mad that I had 5,000 bumper stickers made up that said 'Growth Destroys Bluegrass—Forever.' "

Kitty, as even her children call her, fought this kind of "progress" for twenty years in the Woodford County Courthouse until, as she says, "my children reined me in."

The Graddy property today is much smaller than its original 2,000 acres, and a portion of it is protected by conservation easement. Besides Welcome Hall, there are three other early Graddy homes just over the hill, each of them owned by one of Kitty's four children. "We're kind of cursed with old houses," says Kitty.

The original owner of Welcome Hall, John Long, arrived in the region now known as Woodford County in the late 1780s and began construction on the stone center section of his home in 1789, three years before Kentucky became a state. He soon became a successful farmer and, according to the 1810 census, was the owner of fifteen slaves. In 1816, John Long sold the farm to Jesse Graddy. Two centuries and seven generations later, the Graddys are still on the land.

Today, Welcome Hall is primarily a cattle farm—with additional income from tobacco and hay—but in years past the rich land nourished many crops. Whiskey was almost always one of the products of a self-sufficient farm. Corn would have been raised to make it, and the family thinks there was a small distillery on the property. There would also have been cattle, sheep, hogs, horses, and mules.

> " THE GRADDYS GREW HEMP UNTIL 1940, WHEN IT BECAME ILLEGAL,"
> KITTY EXPLAINS. "THE HEMP SEED WAS HARVESTED DOWN IN THE LOWER STABLE,
> WHICH HAS A DOUBLE WALNUT FLOOR PUT TOGETHER WITH PEGS.
> THE SEED WAS SO VALUABLE THAT WHEN THE PODS WERE BROKEN THE SEED COULD
> BE COLLECTED IN THE SPACE BETWEEN THE TWO FLOORS AND NONE WOULD BE LOST.
> THE HEMP WAS MADE INTO ROPE, WHICH WAS USED TO TIE UP BALES OF COTTON
> FROM DOWN SOUTH BEFORE THEY WERE SHIPPED TO ENGLAND. "

"After that, the money crop became tobacco and this was a tobacco farm, which it still is to some degree. That was during a time when alcohol was the big evil and tobacco was just a pleasant pastime," she says with a wry grin.

A hundred years ago, Welcome Hall was about to be sold at auction because of the financial mismanagement of William Lee Graddy—"an SOB who chased women and foxes," according to Kitty. Instead, his son—Kitty's father-in-law—bought the property with the help of a relative on condition that there be no alcohol at Welcome Hall as long as he lived.

"My parents-in-law were very different," Kitty observes with obvious fondness. "They lived in two different worlds. Mrs. Graddy was a preservationist. She loved flowers and was a wonderful gardener. Mr. Graddy was a farmer and a stockman and one of the last mule breeders in the country. He lived on cornbread and clabber and couldn't tell one flower from another. He put a big trough up on the avenue and filled it with slop from the distillery down the road for his cattle to feed on. It almost caused a divorce. The mash had a very strong smell. It didn't look very good, either."

Kitty and Henry raised their four children at Greenwood, on the hill next to Welcome Hall. The kids could stand watching their father on a tractor in one field, their grandfather behind a team of mules in the next. They would wake in the morning not to the crowing of roosters but to the braying of jackasses.

PISGAH CHURCH

Kitty's in-laws had a profound influence on their eight grandchildren, seven of whom grew up to be farmers and/or gardeners. The exception, Hank Graddy, lives and practices law in the tiny town of Midway, 15 miles away. "All of us loved this place as children," he says. "It was our playground. We would ride our tricycles around the brick pathways."

Even as a high school student, Hank Graddy knew he would someday make a living with his mouth. "I knew I liked to argue," he says, "I knew I liked to advocate, and I knew I didn't want to be a farmer." Today, Hank is one of the top environmental lawyers in the state. Most of his work is related to water quality and land use. Since 1978 he has been involved in litigation that has helped Woodford County become one of the most protected planning and zoning systems of any in Kentucky.

"My love of land," he says, "came from Grandmother. She was an ardent preservationist, involved in restoring Liberty Hall, the Orlando Brown House, and the Pisgah Church down the road. And she was a member of the Audubon Society. She would sit for hours with me when I was little and show me the bird book."

PISGAH PIKE

66

MY COMMITMENT TO WELCOME HALL AND TO OUR LAND HELPED ME
GO INTO LAW SCHOOL KNOWING THAT I WAS GOING TO USE MY DEGREE
TO PROTECT WHAT WE HAVE BEEN GIVEN," HE SAYS,

"TO PROTECT THIS FARM AGAINST BEING SUBDIVIDED, EITHER INTERNALLY

OR EXTERNALLY BY FORCES COMING AT US, AND I WAS GOING TO FIND OTHER

WAYS TO PROTECT FARMING AS I THINK IT SHOULD BE. 99

—Hank Graddy

As a law student, Hank was determined to stay close to home. His opportunities as a young lawyer were in planning and zoning cases that allowed him to oppose the indiscriminate subdividing of farmland. "The thirty-acre minimum-lot size, the agricultural preserve—those are things that Libby Jones fought for, and I fought with Libby as part of Woodford Save the Land. When Libby led the fight to prevent a 725-acre farm from becoming a five-acre development, that created an organization that has done more than any to protect Woodford County.

"Although we can't prove it, I maintain that the reason we have attracted and kept horsemen such as Robert Clay and Will Farish and others here in Woodford County is that they know this is a safe place to invest millions of dollars in horse farms."

Hank cites three reasons why Welcome Hall has remained intact over the years—luck, love of the land, and determination—starting with his grandfather's efforts to repair the family reputation, which had been so badly tarnished by William Lee. "That set the stage for Kitty and Father to try and make farming work. And I believe that all my siblings have a similar determination—to explore every option and not to consider cashing in, dividing things up, and going elsewhere. There has always been a degree of stubbornness in Graddys."

THE GARDEN AT WELCOME HALL
A Smithsonian Garden

The present formula for managing the finances of the farm is the work of Hank's sister. Lucy Graddy Smith stands five foot two, with aquamarine eyes that match her jeans. She is soft-spoken but strong and focused, and at one time she owned and operated the largest flower-producing business in the state. According to Hank, she is in charge of "who owes what now, who gets what now, how bills get paid, where cattle income goes, who is the landlord, who is the grower." She also has what Hank describes as a "deep love" for Welcome Hall.

"Father," Lucy remembers, "would drop me off at Welcome Hall when he was going off to breed mares, so I spent a lot of time there. The garden was a place of magic. And Grandmother, as she gardened, would teach me. She would use the botanical name for every flower."

 THE GARDEN WAS A PLACE OF MAGIC. AND GRANDMOTHER, AS SHE GARDENED, WOULD TEACH ME. SHE WOULD USE THE BOTANICAL NAME FOR EVERY FLOWER.

—Lucy Graddy Smith

The Graddy siblings' commitment to Welcome Hall derives in part from their sense that the farm came to them with an obligation, a kind of trust that it would be taken care of. The hope, according to Hank, is that "Welcome Hall and Greenwood will remain Graddy family farms, and that along with what Lucy owns at Springside and what Joe owns over the next hill at Homestead, they will remain family farms into the future. We are working on how to make that happen. We are negotiating how much of it can we accomplish in our generation, and how much to set the stage for the next generation to try to figure out. What binding decisions do we make today that will affect them? These matters are in flux."

At the same time, all-important questions about the future of farming loom. "It is hard to see much progress since I graduated from law school in 1975," admits Hank. "Regrettably, most of the movement has been in the direction of industrial agriculture—away from family farming and small independent farmers and toward farmers who have basically sold their souls to a company. And so farming has evolved in a terrible direction. But I think things are changing… I believe that with the end of cheap energy we will see a renaissance of locally produced food supplying urban areas. The fact that we have kept some land in production in Kentucky bodes well for our future economy…. This is the time to hold on to the land as best we can and try to ride out into a new economic paradigm where farmers are properly paid for what they produce."

While the family struggles to address practical questions large and small, Lucy speaks to the heart of their effort when she talks about the concept of roots—and sense of place. "When I married and moved away, Father said to me, 'Central Kentucky women always come back—with or without their husbands.' That was his parting shot as we headed over the hill. My husband had a successful practice as an equine vet in Florida, and we were perfectly happy there, with no intention whatsoever of moving back. But he became allergic to horses and had to sell his practice. And so when he said, 'Where do we go?' I said, 'Take… Me… Home.'"

JOE, CAMPBELL, HANK, KITTY, LUCY AND "ELLA"

GREEN JUSTICE

When Hank Graddy was fresh out of law school, he used part of his first paycheck to become a member of the Sierra Club. He has been serving the organization ever since. Much of his work addresses the role of industrial agriculture in global climate change, water and air pollution, and justice issues.

He fought hard to get the Sierra Club to recognize confined animal feeding operations (CAFOs) as a major environmental problem, an effort that led to the Healthy Foods, Local Farms Conference started by the Sierra Club's Kentucky CAFO program ten years ago.

Watershed Watch in Kentucky, a statewide water-monitoring project that he helped organize, became the model for the Sierra Club Water Sentinels Program; and as chair of a national Sierra Club action team, he is tackling the nitrogen and phosphorus pollution that originates in farm states like Kentucky and contributes to the Gulf of Mexico hypoxia zone known as "the Dead Zone."

> "But I think things are changing. This is the time to hold on to the land as best we can and try to ride out into a new economic paradigm where farmers are properly paid for what they produce."
>
> —Hank Graddy

SUNDAY MORNING

CONTEMPORARY CONSERVATION

In 1995, Laura Lee Brown and Steve Wilson bought the thousand-acre Egger farm, a beautiful piece of land high above the Ohio River in Oldham County. They named it Woodland. Two years later they established a breeding farm on the premises for premium American bison. Because Woodland had been continuously farmed for over 150 years, it became the largest single Kentucky property named to the National Registry of Historic Places.

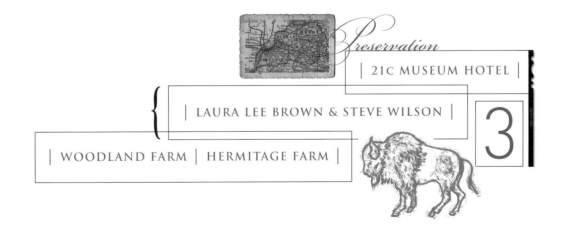

Preservation

| 21C MUSEUM HOTEL |

{ | LAURA LEE BROWN & STEVE WILSON |

3

| WOODLAND FARM | HERMITAGE FARM |

A few years later the couple purchased a handful of historic buildings on Main Street in downtown Louisville and turned them into a contemporary art museum set within a new boutique hotel—the first museum hotel in America. Known as 21c, the property was named by Conde Nast Traveler's 2009 Readers Choice Awards as the best hotel in the United States and the sixth best in the world.

While Woodland Farm and 21c might seem like unrelated enterprises, they reflect the shared passions of the two people who created them. The couple met in 1994 and found themselves drawn together by mutual interests—art, travel, culture, and good food. They also shared a love of the land.

Laura Lee Brown grew up in a gracious white farmhouse on the Ohio River just east of Louisville, and like a lot of the young and privileged, she and her two younger siblings probably took a lot for granted. Sutherland encompassed three hundred acres of rolling Kentucky farmland; short-horned cattle grazed in the fields, and the gardens were designed by Frederick Law Olmsted. "I led a charmed life," says the granddaughter of Brown-Forman founder George Garvin Brown, with a hint of sarcasm. "We had the woods to roam, ponies to ride, swans to chase, and a big marsh in front of the house that held great fascination for us because we were told that it had once absorbed a man on a tractor."

Years after the three Brown children married and moved on, their mother died, and in 1983 the siblings, realizing that the farm was more than any of them could handle, sold Sutherland. Two years later, it sold again, but this time only one hundred acres of the farm went with the house. The remaining two hundred acres were sold to a developer, houses were built, and the marsh was dredged into a lake.

UNTITLED, 2006
WERNER REITERER
Site-specific installation
commissioned for the
21c Museum Hotel.
Brass chandelier,
50 LED lights, gallows pole,
megaphone, sound

"I guess you'd have to say that a big part of this story is that Laura Lee always regretted what had happened to Sutherland," says Steve. "Back then, I don't think she or her siblings had any idea of what could happen to it. Development was just beginning to move out that way—and Sutherland had always been a farm, and therefore it would always be a farm. The family sold it all in one piece, with no concept that it could be subdivided but also with no understanding of how to protect it."

Steve Wilson grew up on his family farm as well, in Ballard County, at the western tip of the state. "We raised corn, soybeans, pigs, and cattle," he says, "and I couldn't wait to get out of there. My plan was to go to college and then to the big city—and do something important."

Despite the fact that he wanted to get out as fast as he could, Steve had a fairly extensive background in farming. Active in 4-H throughout his youth, he proved to be a born leader, becoming state vice-president at sixteen.

Self-confident and not shy about being the center of attention, Steve once rode a horse all the way to the state fair in Louisville, a distance of three hundred miles, to raise public awareness for 4-H. "My father said I couldn't do it," he says.

While at Murray State University, Steve spent time in Thailand on an agricultural exchange, and when he graduated, he began working in politics. He stayed in Frankfort "too long," he says—through four governors—and was director of special projects for governors John Y. Brown and Wallace G. Wilkinson.

Helen and George Egger's farm consisted of one thousand acres, several farmhouses, and a main house, which had been built during the 1830s and commanded a breathtaking view of the Ohio River. It also included the 130-acre Wood Island just off the Kentucky shore. "The Eggers were always sort of mythical people," says Laura Lee. "People would talk about that land out there—about going out for beagle hunts. It always seemed like a place we needed to see. Then we heard it was for sale."

As Steve tells it: "I met a mutual friend at the telephone-book dump in the parking lot at Kroger, and she had the brochure in her hand. It showed that the farm was being promoted as a golfing community—a thousand acres."

" I REMEMBER DRIVING DOWN THAT LONG DRIVEWAY FOR THE FIRST TIME,
IT WAS SPRING. THE WILD COLUMBINE WAS IN BLOOM. "

—Laura Lee Brown

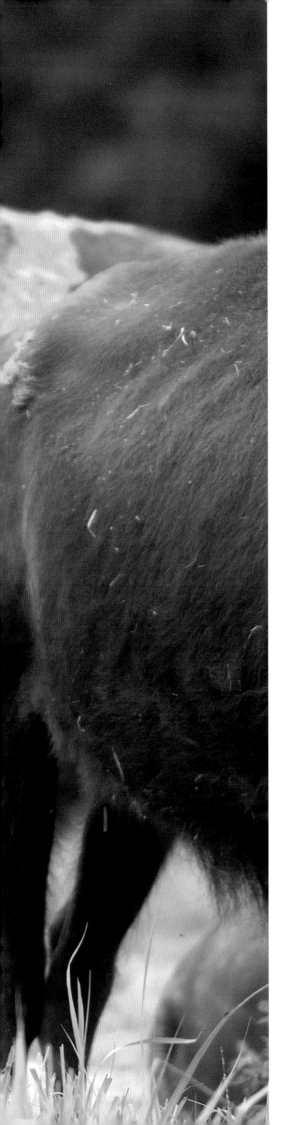

"I remember driving down that long driveway for the first time," says Laura Lee. "It was spring. The wild columbine was in bloom."

The first thing Steve and Laura Lee did after buying the Eggers property was to take steps to keep it from ever being subdivided. That left another challenge. "Basically we bought the farm," says Steve, "and then we had to decide what we were going to do with it."

Turning the huge piece of property into a working farm took considerable ingenuity. "We looked at Thoroughbreds and ostrich and beef," says Steve. "But we didn't like the hormone implants in beef, and thank God we didn't go into ostrich. We knew that buffalo were something not many farmers would try. Buffalo had at one time been on the endangered list. We liked the idea of preserving the breed—helping to bring it back. We found that romantic. But most of all we liked the idea that buffalo had healthy meat." Buffalo, he adds, live longer than cattle and calve without help. They require no growth hormones or stimulants and are naturally more disease-resistant than most domestic livestock. Their meat has almost no fat. The disadvantage is that they have a flight-or-flight defense mechanism.

 YOU CAN HERD A BUFFALO ANYWHERE HE WANTS TO GO.

—Steve Wilson

"We had twenty-two head of buffalo on the farm the day we were married. We put grain down on the driveway so they would be out there to greet people! I guess we thought we'd live happily ever after on this great big thousand-acre farm where the buffalo would roam and we'd sit and look at them. As it turned out, it's a lot more difficult than that.

"One time someone left a gate open and the whole herd got out. There were sixteen yearling bulls, so it was like teenagers out for the first time. They went swimming in the river, and someone from Westport called and said, 'Your buffalo are in the river.' Eventually, they swam back to the farm. Then they went up through the valley and crossed US 42 at the Clore farm—where they saw cows for the first time in their lives. So there wasn't much left of that fence. That was at dusk, so we fed them there, because we definitely didn't want them to move at night. Buffalo are afraid of their own shadows—the slightest little thing can make them stampede. We hoped to keep them still until the school buses passed by in the morning, but as soon as it got light they started moving again. We had state police, the health department, weather helicopters, animal control, traffic stopped, school buses stopped. We finally got them herded into a neighbor's farm."

In 1999, Steve and Laura Lee purchased five buildings in an area of Main Street that used to be called Distillery Row. Downtown Louisville was experiencing a rejuvenation, and the couple wanted to be a part of it. The buildings—dilapidated warehouses and a bank—dated from the late 1800s and were listed on the National Register of Historic Places. "It was a little bit like buying the farm," said Laura Lee. "We bought the buildings, and then we had to decide what to do with them. We looked at things that were needed—things that would make other things happen downtown: a grocery, condominiums, a hotel."

Steve and Laura Lee's beautifully restored two-hundred-year-old brick farmhouse is filled with contemporary art they have collected. It is everywhere—sometimes playful, sometimes shocking, and always thought provoking. A couple of life-size camels serve as living-room couches, and a huge stone rabbit naps under a table in the library. Friends arriving for cocktails may be greeted by the mechanical figure of an Asian businessman—hat and all—crawling toward them across the chestnut floor of the front hallway.

The couple believes art is a good economic booster and that a thriving art scene is critical for cities that are trying to draw people back downtown. "We thought about how much fun it is for people to visit us at our home and experience our art," says Laura Lee, "and what it might be like to introduce lots of people to that experience in a public place." Thus was born 21c, a ninety-room hotel that celebrates twenty-first century art—the only hotel and museum in America dedicated to living artists, open twenty-four hours a day, and free. "Nobody thought it could work," says Steve.

Teaming up with Louisville lawyer Craig Greenberg, the couple had the buildings integrated into a seamless hotel design by New York–based architect Deborah Berke, whom Steve describes as "well known for her minimalist style. The preservationists wanted the raw brick walls of the warehouses left that way, and Deborah had a lot of experience making an old building contemporary."

CLOUD MACHINES, 2006
NED KAHN
Site-specific installation
commissioned for the
21c Museum Hotel.

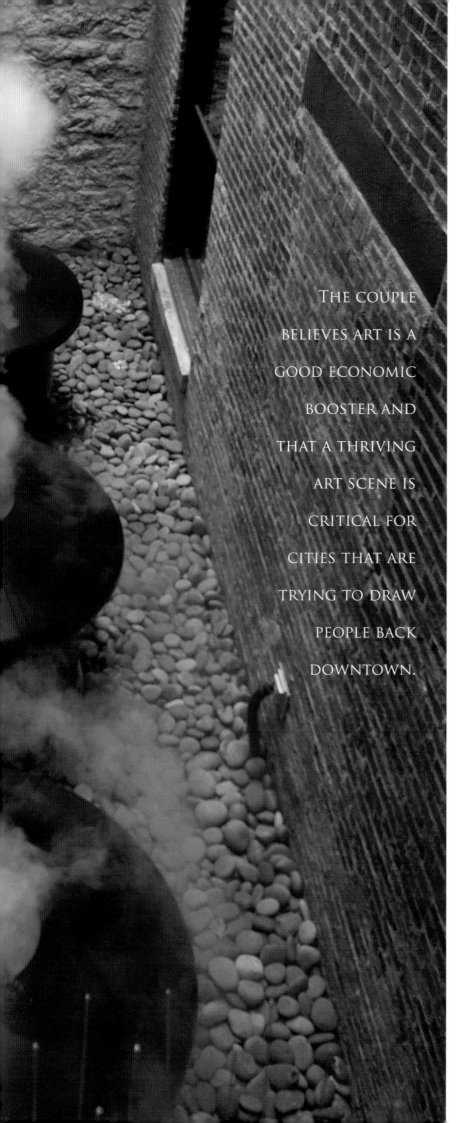

THE COUPLE
BELIEVES ART IS A
GOOD ECONOMIC
BOOSTER AND
THAT A THRIVING
ART SCENE IS
CRITICAL FOR
CITIES THAT ARE
TRYING TO DRAW
PEOPLE BACK
DOWNTOWN.

A substantial portion of the $26 million price tag was financed by Steve and Laura Lee themselves, with major help from grants, tax credits, and other government incentives.

The finished space includes more than nine thousand square feet of exhibit space and the restaurant and bar Proof on Main, which fills the front corner of the hotel and was picked by Esquire magazine as one of the twenty best new restaurants of 2006, the year it opened. The museum exhibits the work of rising and established local and international artists, most from Laura Lee and Steve's own collection.

The art that vibrates 21c is definitely not what one thinks of as hotel art (and not everyone's cup of tea, either). There are, for example, the four-foot-tall red plastic penguins acquired on a trip to Venice in 2005. The birds have become accidental mascots for the hotel, lining its rooftop and showing up in unexpected places all over the building—seated in the restaurant, riding the elevator. The current flock numbers thirty-eight—one bird light, since someone made off with a penguin last year.

With plans afoot to replicate 21c in other cities, more penguins have been ordered up. "Every now and then," Laura Lee says, her dimple showing, "we get a letter with a photograph" depicting the whereabouts of the missing bird. "The first one was about how he hated to leave the flock but needed to see the world. He was standing on a beach with the ocean behind him. The last one came from somewhere in France."

With its mix of Kentucky hospitality, historic buildings, and the stunning art of confident collectors, the hotel at the corner of Seventh and Main not only adds immeasurably to the soul of the city but may even have a salutary effect on the countryside as well.

BIG GREEN RABBITS, 2009
CRACKING ART GROUP
Commissioned for the collection
of Laura Lee Brown and Steve Wilson.
Woodland Farm
Plastic

> ❝ THE INTERESTING THING TO REMEMBER IS THAT BEFORE WORLD WAR II, ALL FARMS WERE DIVERSIFIED— THEY ALL WERE SELF-SUFFICIENT. SO HERE AT WOODLAND, WE'RE REALLY RETURNING TO A LIFESTYLE THAT WAS ONCE THE BACKBONE OF AMERICA. ❞
>
> —Steve Wilson

"Ultimately," Steve says, "it's still part of our efforts to preserve farmland, because if we can make the core of our cities more vibrant and attractive to live in, then it will be less attractive to drive to the suburbs and build a house in the middle of a field."

There are now roughly five hundred head of buffalo at Woodland Farm, and the business has expanded to include more property and more bison grazing directly across the river. The couple plans for all of their land to eventually be protected under conservation easement. "We didn't buy that land just for the view," says Laura Lee, emotion creeping into her voice. "We planned on raising buffalo over there. But so much of the glory of this farm is what you see across the river—and that will never change."

Today, the Kentucky Bison Company is doing very well under the management of Steve's son, J. B. Wilson, who started as a farmhand when the company was incorporated in 1995. The meat is sold to local restaurants, groceries, and at farmers' markets and is distributed from the company's own building on East Main Street in Louisville. While there are a few customers in southern Indiana, Cincinnati, and Tennessee, the company has intentionally kept most of its business local—helped by the acquisition of a former beef and pork processing plant in southern Indiana. That facility, says Steve, is also valuable to other local farmers because small processing plants are disappearing and the ones remaining are mostly too far away.

"We were really lucky," says Steve. "The fact that we were able to buy it and process our own meat was a great help to us. It's an example of value-added farming—cutting out the middleman. Historically, that's been the main reason the farmer gets so little for his product: The middleman gets a big chunk."

With J. B. Wilson running the Kentucky Bison Company and other professionals running the hotel, Steve has had more time to get back to the farm, and as a result, more and more of the fabulous food served at Proof on Main comes straight from there.

"We are diversifying the farm," Steve says. "We've learned a lot about the sustainable food movement, and people coming in the restaurant want local food, so we decided we needed to provide more local products from the farm." That means tons of varieties of heirloom tomatoes—and radishes and lettuces—for the chefs at Proof. It means apples, peaches, pears, and cherries from the orchard. It means sweet corn in season and dry corn to send down the road to the Weisenberger Mill to be ground into meal. "We're raising hogs for home-cured ham, bacon and sausages," says Steve, "and chickens for eggs."

The exchange between farm and restaurant works the other way, too: A small refinery on the property converts cooking oil from the restaurant to bio fuel, which powers all of the tractors on the farm.

"The interesting thing to remember is that before World War II, all farms were diversified—they all were self-sufficient. So here at Woodland, we're really returning to a lifestyle that was once the backbone of America."

PHOTOGRAPHS
SEPTEMBERIST SERIES
EXHIBITED IN PROOF ON MAIN
from left
SLEEPING, 2007
GREENHOUSE, 2007
ANTHONY GOICOLEA
C-prints on aluminum

SCULPTURES
RED PENGUINS, 2005
CRACKING ART GROUP
Originally commissioned for the
2005 Venice Biennale.
21c acquired 50 of original
250 Red Penguins in conjunction
with the grand opening in 2006.
Plastic

DRIVING AT HERMITAGE

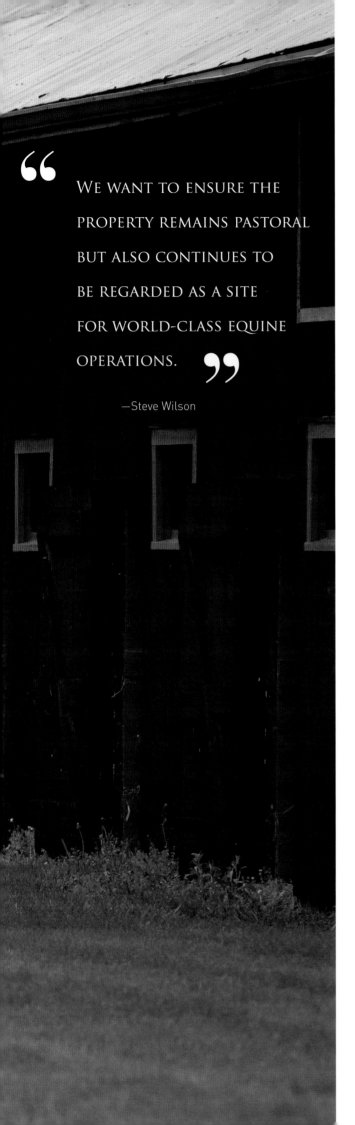

" WE WANT TO ENSURE THE PROPERTY REMAINS PASTORAL BUT ALSO CONTINUES TO BE REGARDED AS A SITE FOR WORLD-CLASS EQUINE OPERATIONS. "

—Steve Wilson

HERMITAGE, ca 1835.
An unusual Antebellum home with a mix of
Georgian and Federal design—and two front doors.

In the summer of 2010, Laura Lee and Steve bought Hermitage Farm, the Oldham County Thoroughbred broodmare farm established in 1935 by the late Warner Jones. With its signature black fencing and red-trimmed barns, Hermitage is one of the most beautiful farms in Kentucky, and under the charismatic horseman it became one of the most successful as well. After Jones' death, his good friend Carl Pollard bought the farm from the family, retained all of the Hermitage employees, and continued to operate the thriving breeding operation for the next fifteen years. As Pollard began to consider options for the farm's future for estate-planning reasons, Laura Lee and Steve quickly stepped in.

"Were Hermitage to ever be developed," says Laura Lee, "it would upset the balance of green along the main thoroughfare in Oldham County. To have that farm vanish would be unthinkable."

Therefore, the couple is working with architects and equine industry leaders to chart a long-term plan for the farm and will place its nearly seven hundred acres under a conservation easement. That goes against traditional wisdom, which says that if a landowner is to protect himself and his heirs, he must retain his development rights.

"We want to ensure the property remains pastoral but also continues to be regarded as a site for world-class equine operations," says Steve. "Many people believe that if they put their farm in easement it devalues the land. But Randell Arendt, the nation's leading authority on conservation design, has proven that in many states, including Kentucky, it creates value. If we can save this land and show what can be done . . . "

PENTHOUSE GARDEN
21c MUSEUM HOTEL, LOUISVILLE
GARDEN DESIGN BY JON CARLOFTIS

AVANT-GARDENER

Arriving in Manhattan "fresh out of college and green as grass," Jon Carloftis started his garden design business twenty years ago in the laid-back fashion that for him is typical: "I made up some cards that said 'Jon Carloftis, Rooftop Gardener' and gave them out to the doormen and elevator operators all along the Upper East Side. I said, 'Give them to the people on top.' Of course, I'd never been on a rooftop in my life—but I'd looked up and seen plenty of them. One of the cards happened to get to an art collector and her husband. They called me, and that was the beginning."

Garden
| JON CARLOFTIS |
{ | ON THE ROCKCASTLE RIVER |
4

PRIVATE TRIBECA
PENTHOUSE GARDEN
GARDEN DESIGN
BY JON CARLOFTIS,
Photo by Helen Norman,
Courtesy of Jon Carloftis

Prominent New York families were enchanted by the young man with the soft Southern drawl who charmed them with his love of physical labor and his passion to make things beautiful. And who did things differently.

"I didn't plan on it being different," Jon says. "I just did what I did, and people ended up liking it."

Today, the Kentucky gardener who took his talent to the rooftop terraces of New York City, turning a few dozen square feet into intimate and magical garden rooms, is known throughout the United States as a garden designer, writer, and lecturer. Jon Carloftis is the author of four books, has been featured in myriad magazines, and sits on the advisory board of HGTV, but you won't find his name in the New York City phone directory. Not now—maybe never. His flourishing business is all word of mouth. More important, he is beloved by his clients.

> " Despite the splash he has made in the Big Apple and beyond—with such well-known clients as Julianne Moore, Edward Norton and Mike Myers—Jon's heart and soul are in Kentucky, where, he says, 'I was raised by Momma and Daddy in a beautiful place.' And more than anything, he says, 'I love comin' home.' "

—Jon Carloftis

FORT SEQUOYAH ca 1960
Photo Courtesy of Lucille Carloftis

Home for Jon is and always has been an almost over-the-rainbow kind of place deep in the foothills of the Appalachian Mountains of eastern Kentucky, where, he says, "In 1955, Momma and Daddy started their business: a tourist stop for people traveling the Dixie Highway."

But it was much more than that. In the old days, the American countryside was dotted with small family-owned diners and roadside attractions. Families took road trips and vacations along two-lane highways, and back then, the Carloftis property on Highway 25 was on the main route from Michigan to Florida. Jon's parents, Lucille and Carlos Carloftis, had a dream.

"We had traveled many times to Cherokee, North Carolina," Lucille recalls, "where there was an Indian reservation. And we became so enthralled with the Native American culture. We saw the work that these people did, and we appreciated it so much. We thought how wonderful it would be to be able to introduce others to their beautiful ways. If we hadn't been so young, we would never have thought that."

They decided to build a tourist stop: an Indian village. It would be an exact replica of the reservation at Cherokee—a re-creation of a village of the mid-1700s. The couple found a small stretch of land near the tiny town of Livingston. Fifty acres of natural beauty, it was surrounded by the Daniel Boone National Forest and bordered on one side by the lazy Rockcastle River and on the other by the heavily traveled Highway 25. "It was just waiting for us," says Lucille.

Carlos built a home beside the river and, when it was complete, brought his family from their very comfortable life in nearby Pineville to this wild and rugged place where there was no electricity, no telephone, and no running water. Lucille would later comment, "Both sets of our parents made it clear that they thought we had lost our minds."

"When my parents first came here," says the youngest Carloftis daughter, Betsy, "I was only six weeks old, and it was so rough and wild. Momma would go down and get water from the creek, and drive that International truck and shift all those gears, and Granny and Great-Granny would not let them bring me over here. So I stayed in Pineville with my grandparents until I was six months old—in my diapers, which were starched."

JON & SAM LOSSIAH (CHIEF LIGHTFOOT) ca 1968
Photo Courtesy of Jon Carloftis

Aided by their good friends from Cherokee, whom they had befriended over time, Carlos designed and built the Indian village and named it Fort Sequoyah. Lucille remembers, "We opened on July 2, 1955, and at the end of the day we had cleared eight dollars. And I thought, "What have we done?"" But the business became a huge success.

Sometimes during the tourist season, there were as many as thirty Native Americans living at Fort Sequoyah. A day pass would allow visitors to step back in time—to walk through and see living history. There were women cooking and making clothes. There was basket weaving, pottery making, and beading. There was a silversmith from Acoma, New Mexico, who made beautiful jewelry. At the end, visitors would be led into the Council House to hear the story of the Trail of Tears.

"We had a rustic museum here, which Carlos built. It had a fabulous collection of artifacts," says Lucille. "And then there was the store. We had one of the finest Indian stores in the country, because after we got started, we would travel to reservations all over the country and bring back beautiful things.

"We didn't have a telephone for years. I'd go up the hill to the Laurel Lodge five or six miles away and call in the orders for the week."

Betsy says, "When I was five years old, Granny was afraid I'd get stolen, because cars were parked out on the highway from one end to the other, two deep. And when we weren't playing down by the river swinging on vines, or in the village with Walking Stick or Miss Betty, all of us would dart in and out of those cars, putting on bumper stickers. And my grandparents would say it's a wonder we hadn't gotten killed; it's a wonder we hadn't gotten stolen. And Momma and Daddy would be working, and we wouldn't see them for a long time, but then Daddy would whistle and we'd come— like the Von Trapp family. And he'd count us. That must have happened twenty times a day. We'd gather up—stand at attention—he'd look at us and make sure we were safe. When you heard Daddy's whistle, you knew you'd better get in there."

 OUR CHILDREN RAN WILD ALL OVER THIS PLACE. THEY DIDN'T KNOW WHETHER THEY WERE TOM SAWYER OR HUCKLEBERRY FINN. BUT I WILL HAVE TO SAY THAT BY TODAY'S STANDARDS, THEY REALLY HAD A VERY SIMPLE LIFE. AND I'M GRATEFUL FOR THAT.

—Lucille Carloftis

In 1970, Fort Sequoyah expanded, and a replica of a western town of the 1850s was added. With a general store, a jail, a saloon, a blacksmith shop, and a shoot-'em-up every day at high noon, there was even more fun to be had along Highway 25. Families made it a regular stop, prompting one couple to recount that their children "started asking—back in Nebraska—'When will we be there?' "

Lucille, says Jon, "woke up to be with people."

"Where are you from?" she would ask. And that would be the start of it: making visitors feel welcome, introducing them to one another—"making music," she called it.

"Our children ran wild all over this place. They didn't know whether they were Tom Sawyer or Huckleberry Finn. But I will have to say that by today's standards, they really had a very simple life. And I'm grateful for that," says Lucille.

With no TV to watch and with the family's closest neighbors miles away, the six Carloftis children played in the woods: fished for bluegill, swung on vines down by the river, sewed vests out of the giant elephant-ear plants, and were at home in the natural playground of the forest. Their childhood friends were Cherokee, and their lives were intertwined with the steady stream of visitors and tourists who stopped there every day.

Jon would often accompany his father along the path beside the river to the spring—a mile away—to check the pump that brought water to their cistern. "All along the way, he'd teach me about the trees: 'Look how sycamores only grow at the river bottom, not up high. That's just where they love it. This is a sweet bay magnolia… this is a hemlock… this is a Christmas fern.' " By the time he was a teenager, Jon knew most of the names of the native trees, shrubs, and flowers that grew along the path, never dreaming he'd make a career out of it.

After graduating from the University of Kentucky with a degree in communications and suffering through a couple of office jobs—"air-conditioned, under fluorescent lighting"—he went back to school to study horticulture. "I decided I was going to do what I really love. Gardening. I just wanted to take a space and make it beautiful." And that's what he did.

Today, Jon's home-and-garden store, the Rockcastle River Trading Company, stands on the same stone foundation that once held the old Fort Sequoyah Trading Post, and with it, a little slice of New York City has come to the mountains of eastern Kentucky. Although Highway 25 is sleepy in comparison to the old days, when cars were parked bumper to bumper, there is a steady stream of customers through the front door. And with the help of the Internet, business is booming.

"

THE REASON I BOUGHT THAT OLD CADDY...
IT WAS THE SAME KIND AND COLOR AS
THE ONE THAT MOMMA AND DADDY
DROVE TO THE ROCKCASTLE BACK IN 1955.
CAN YOU IMAGINE LEAVING THE FINEST HOUSE
IN PINEVILLE, LOADING UP THE NEW CADILLAC
AND MOVING TO THE RIVER TO START A NEW
LIFE? BUT WE ALL MARCH TO A DIFFERENT
DRUMMER AND I DIDN'T EVEN THINK TWICE
ABOUT MOVING TO THE CITY AND STARTING
A BUSINESS FROM SCRATCH. IN RETROSPECT,
THANK GOODNESS THAT IT ALL TURNED
OUT ALRIGHT... IF WE HAD THOUGHT
ABOUT IT LONG ENOUGH...

"

—Jon Carloftis

"Dusty," Betsy, Carcille, Lucille and "Buzz"

The store, which is run by Lucille with the help of daughter Betsy and son Buzz, is filled with wondrous things: whimsical statues and fountains, rare species of trees, pottery and linens and pewter tableware with names like Vietri and Peacock Alley and Match. There are hand-milled soaps from France stacked next to quart jars of deep amber honey from the local beekeeper. And there are magazines featuring stories about Jon Carloftis—dozens of them: *Martha Stewart Living*, for example, and *Country Gardens* and *Metropolitan Home*. But with all of that, things are very low-key. The Carloftis children and their children, except for Jon, live close by—they are easy here. Checking in—greeting people, telling stories—it's still home. "What I'm so happy about," Lucille will tell you, "is that all of my children love to come home. I think they feel ownership of this place and what went on here."

Jon is spending more time in Kentucky these days, tending to projects all over the state—"my Kentucky gardens," he calls them. He returns home every month to rearrange the store, change light bulbs, move trees, tend to the garden, and to cook and unwind." This is home," he explains. "I come down here to get away from everything. My cell phone doesn't work down here."

And so there'll be lamb roast, kale greens, and cornbread. Buzz will have fetched a neighbor or two over for dinner on the deck. And Lucille's soft voice can be heard talking with a young couple in the store: asking where they're from, introducing them to others, making music, as she says.

COMEBACK STORY

In its day, Bloomfield was a small but thriving farm town in rural Nelson County. There were two tobacco markets and the D. B. Sutherland Mill, and the L&N stopped for passengers at the depot every morning at precisely one minute before noon. During the weeks that the tobacco markets were open, farmers flooded the town, their pockets filled with cash from their labors, and business was good all over.

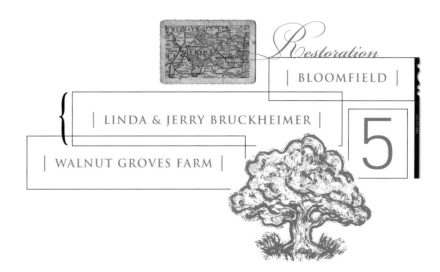

Restoration

| BLOOMFIELD |

{ | LINDA & JERRY BRUCKHEIMER |

| WALNUT GROVES FARM |

5

Established in 1790 and incorporated in 1819, the town was settled by early pioneers who, as they headed west, found what they were looking for: a verdant landscape ripe for farming. Constructed mostly between the mid-1800s and early 1900s, Bloomfield through the years was able to hold onto much of its original architectural charm, and in 1991 the town was listed in the National Register of Historic Places. Adding to its charm was Simpson Creek, which ran right through the center of town, as it does today, under the front porch of the Wells Building, under Taylorsville Road, and out the other side where Charlie Tingle's Used Car Lot used to be.

But like small towns across America, Bloomfield declined as its economy slowly leached into the surrounding suburbs, and by the time the train was long gone and the strip malls had done their work, downtown Bloomfield was barely holding onto its history, much less its dignity. And that's where Linda Bruckheimer and her husband, Jerry, entered the picture.

A fifth-generation Kentuckian, Linda was raised in Louisville but moved with her family to Los Angeles as a teenager. She became the West Coast editor for *Mirabella* magazine, the writer-producer of two award-winning PBS specials, and the author of two novels, *Dreaming Southern* and *The Southern Belles of Honeysuckle Way*. Along the way, she married Jerry Bruckheimer, one of Hollywood's most successful producers. But despite her vibrant California lifestyle, Linda's heart was in Kentucky, and after years of absence, she longed for her roots.

"Each time I returned to Louisville to visit my grandmother," she recalls, "I would travel the back roads of the countryside, sometimes leaving early in the morning and not returning until midnight. I fell in love with every bit of it, from the antebellum architecture to the old barns to the one-horse towns."

Linda will tell you emphatically that she did not plan on buying a block of a town and fixing it up. "Definitely not," she says, "and I'm pretty sure my husband didn't either." In 1994 she and Jerry bought Walnut Groves Farm, a bucolic piece of property just outside the tiny town of Bloomfield, population 845. Gradually, as she learned about the heritage of the town and got to know its people, something happened. "It all unfolded organically," she says. "One thing led to another—I fell in love."

The town has become a destination for Kentuckians and out-of-state tourists alike. Nettie Jarvis Antiques, named for Linda's great-grandmother, is a main attraction in downtown Bloomfield. The building has been carefully returned to its turn-of-the-century splendor. Inside, the dark oak floors shine; the woodwork is thick, lush, and gleaming; antiques from the late eighteenth and early nineteenth centuries are artfully arranged.

First, the couple purchased a former dry goods store built by the Wells family in 1899. "There were broken windows and trash cans catching the water," recalls Jenny Wigginton, a Bloomfield native and Linda's longtime assistant. "That's how bad it was." That was in 1997. Today the restored Wells Building houses a shop that sells "Primitives," according to the handsome sign in front: "Furniture, folk art, quilts and accessories."

The building that currently houses Nettie Jarvis Antiques once served as a pool hall and was in even worse shape. "The windows were boarded up, the upstairs floors had collapsed, and raccoons had taken over," says Jenny.

Delighted with the results the work was yielding, Linda continued to buy and restore buildings one by one, consulting with the town's citizens, the Kentucky Heritage Council (which serves as the state's historic preservation office), and other state and local advisors to determine what the historic downtown could and should be. For Linda, who serves on the board of trustees of the National Trust for Historic Preservation, this kind of work was like throwing Br'er Rabbit into the briar patch.

Once the ball got rolling, others were inspired to fix up their own properties. The Kentucky Heritage Council helped the Bruckheimers receive tax credits for the rehabbed buildings. A grant helped restore the classic 1930s WPA concrete bridge over Simpson Creek. Other projects were on the drawing board. Brick by brick, Bloomfield was coming back.

"Passionate is not nearly a strong enough word to adequately describe Linda's love of Kentucky's history and heritage," says David Morgan, who was director of the Kentucky Heritage Council at the time. "We formed a real partnership with her—not only in Bloomfield but also in preservation activities statewide."

"When I see a bulldozer parked outside a historic building," says Linda, "I pretty much flip. I don't understand the strategy behind knocking down a nineteenth-century courthouse or a church to make way for a parking lot. There's lots of talk about progress. That's not progress. What's more important to Kentuckians than our heritage? We have been given an abundance of treasures and it's a crime to squander them."

Walk down Taylorsville Road—Bloomfield's main street—with Jenny Wigginton and you'll quickly understand how people feel about the changes brought about by Linda's efforts. "Many of these buildings probably wouldn't be here today if it weren't for her," says Jenny.

The town has become a destination for Kentuckians and out-of-state tourists alike. Nettie Jarvis Antiques, named for Linda's great-grandmother, is a main attraction in downtown Bloomfield. The building has been carefully returned to its turn-of-the-century splendor. Inside, the dark oak floors shine; the woodwork is thick, lush, and gleaming; antiques from the late eighteenth and early nineteenth centuries are artfully arranged.

Rooms glitter with shining crystal, case after case of exquisite silver, and everything is perfect right down to the jazz and swing wafting through the building, calling you back to a time when "Laura" and "I Gotta Girl in Kalamazoo" were the hit tunes of the day.

Just across the street, the Olde Bloomfield Meeting Hall has something for everyone: bowling, pool tables, a roller rink, pinball machines, a 1920s fortune-teller. Behind a long bar complete with ice cream stools is a sign that spells out "Ernie's Tavern" in neon. The place is open every Friday and Saturday night for families and kids and can also be rented for special events. Bowling alley, skating rink, dance hall—it's a trip back to a simpler time.

Earnestine Whitehouse works the counter and handles everything from reservations to bowling balls. Earnestine was born in 1929 and moved here when she was seven after her father died, "because all of Mother's people were from this area. And I've been here ever since.

"We serve hot dogs and hot popcorn, and cotton candy," Ernestine says, obviously pleased with her little domain.

"Bloomfield is one of the prime examples of a very small town in Kentucky," says David Morgan. "The architecture is great, the history is great, and you come off a country road right into a real town without passing a strip mall or a Wal-Mart. Thanks to the Bruckheimers' work, Bloomfield is a vital and vibrant community again—and the type of place tourists like to visit."

For Linda, who believes that restoration reaches beyond the floors and ceilings and walls of a building, all the attention given to the Bruckheimers' efforts impacts more than Bloomfield. Ultimately, it is a tool for community pride and revitalization for all Kentuckians.

No GABLING
ALLOWD THIS M
PLEASE DONT SW

THE BUILDING THAT CURRENTLY HOUSES NETTIE
JARVIS ANTIQUES ONCE SERVED AS A POOL HALL

"My husband and I are fortunate enough to have the means to do this," she says. "But the heart of preservation is not in the wallet. You can help preserve something by speaking up. Everyone can write a note or make a phone call. And believe me, I have written my fair share of poison pen letters!"

Linda's love affair with Bloomfield began back when she was driving around the countryside on her visits home; one day she discovered the narrow lane leading to Walnut Groves Farm. At the time, the property comprised fifty-two acres, an 1820 Greek Revival home, a tobacco barn, and a smokehouse. The main house, according to Linda, was in disrepair, "but the architectural details, including the southern pine floors and Egyptian Revival woodwork, were intact—and spectacular."

With great care and much research Linda renovated the house, filling it with a fine collection of Kentucky and American antiques. Then she set about making the place a gracious and relaxing retreat for family and guests. New trees were planted and the ancient ones groomed. She traveled to dozens of historic homes and plantations to learn about early American farm life, paying particular attention to the outbuildings, as well as to the concept of self-sufficiency.

To protect the original homestead and ward off development, the Bruckheimers bought surrounding farmland. Then they began to resuscitate old barns and buildings and add new ones. Relying on the artistry of Kentucky craftsmen, including Bardstown stonemason Jim Bickett, they restored the smokehouse, repaired miles of stone fences, added a stone-edged swimming pool, a round brick cannery for storing vegetables from the garden, and a massive stone carriage house. Decidedly, the most unusual structure on the property is a state-of-the-art hockey rink hidden inside a rustic barn—Jerry Bruckheimer grew up in Michigan and is mad for the sport. "People are pretty shocked when they open those wooden doors and see the ice, the scoreboard, and a locker room," says Linda.

The guesthouses are log cabins found around the state and restored; one belonged to Abraham Lincoln's great-uncle, Richard Berry Jr. Found in Washington County, the Bruckheimers bought it, had it dismantled—each log numbered—and moved to Walnut Groves, where it sits next to a mossy pond.

"When I drove over to Washington County to look at it, I was shocked by the cabin's dilapidated condition," Linda remembers. "It was covered with rotten siding, surrounded by shattered glass, and was on the verge of collapse. Nonetheless, my heart started racing. I turned to a friend and exclaimed, 'Isn't it fantastic?' She thought I was nuts."

No one is more appreciative and proud of Linda's preservation work than her husband. "From the first time I saw Walnut Groves, I loved it," says Jerry Bruckheimer. "It continues to be my favorite place to share with Linda, our daughter, and our friends. When we bought the farm, I couldn't imagine how much work we would end up doing and how much the community would change. When we came here, neither one of us knew a soul. Now we feel like we've lived here all our lives."

Before restoration

THE RICHARD BERRY JR. CABIN
Now a guest house

WHAT'S MORE IMPORTANT TO KENTUCKIANS THAN OUR HERITAGE?

WE HAVE BEEN GIVEN AN ABUNDANCE OF TREASURES

AND IT'S A CRIME TO SQUANDER THEM.

—Linda Bruckheimer

The
Hart
Of The
Matter

The Green River rises in Lincoln County, in south-central Kentucky, then winds its way west, through Edmonson, Barren, LaRue, and Taylor counties—and even through the world's largest underground cave system—until it finally empties into the Ohio, three hundred miles downstream. It is the longest river in Kentucky and, according to the Nature Conservancy, "a national treasure of biodiversity." About a quarter of the way through its journey, the river slices through the heart of Hart County and for a while runs alongside the small town of Munfordville, where the Middleton family lives.

Balance

| APPLE HILL FARM |

{ | DR. JIMMY MIDDLETON |

6

Jimmy Middleton and his wife, Lynn, live on the family farm called Apple Hill. Dr. Middleton practices general medicine along with his pediatrician wife at the Family Medical Center of Hart County, which they built. He also has a Ph.D in agricultural economics. The couple's Victorian cottage, built in 1900 by Jimmy's grandparents, sits in the middle of an apple orchard, and history books will tell you that during the Civil War, that orchard was the site of a Union Army encampment.

Three hundred years ago, the banks of the river here were lush with native grasses, wildflowers, and fine-timbered trees. Buffalo grazed and drank from its waters, and Indians fished and hunted. In time, pioneers settled and built their homes, and a hundred years later, a Civil War battle was fought along the south shore.

Jimmy Middleton's family has lived in Hart County for five generations. His mother was a Hubbard, and the Hubbards started farming the land here 150 years ago. By the turn of the century the Hubbard land included three family farms, which ran along the river. They were significant properties as far as land held in Munfordville in those days, for they took up nearly a third of it. But today the family farms that shaped the culture of families like theirs are disappearing fast. And that bothers Jimmy a lot.

"Our farm people were self-sufficient. They loved the land and made their living from it," Jimmy says. "They'd go out there and work hard all day, and at the end of the day, you could see what you'd done. You'd broken some ground, you'd cut some firewood, you'd castrated your hogs, you'd built a fence—and there's something about that that gives you a feeling of worth and a feeling of accomplishment that we don't have in a lot of our daily living.

"For a long time, tobacco was the lifeblood of farmers here, but when the tobacco program ended, the last thing that was trying to hold the rural farming community together was gone. I have a degree in agricultural economics, and I farm a lot of acres. I struggle with this stuff every day, and I know there is just no way a farmer can survive today practicing traditional farming. But I do think that reestablishing the forest is a way to make a living." So lately, Jimmy—who thinks a lot like Thomas Jefferson and acts a lot like Johnny Appleseed—has been trying to coax the land back to the way it was three hundred years ago, because he believes that's where the future lies. Using a two-pronged approach and with lots of help from a couple of conservation groups, he plants acres of native grasses and thousands of trees on his land. It's important for a lot of reasons, one being the river.

 Look out through there: that's what this country looked like 300 years ago, they claim. That's the real McCoy. 99

—Jimmy Middleton

THE RIVER

According to the Nature Conservancy, the Green River is "one of the top four river systems in the United States in terms of its fish and mussel diversity. Few streams rival the 151 species of fishes and 71 species of freshwater mussels in its system. Among these are a number of endemic species found nowhere else on earth and more than 35 aquatic species that are considered imperiled. The mineral dissolution of the watershed's underlying limestone bedrock makes the Green River a natural companion to nearby Mammoth Cave, the world's largest known underground cave system."

"There's not been a lot of industrialization along the Green," Jimmy explains. "There hasn't been major development, and so it's largely unspoiled. The fact that Hart County has been poor has been a blessing in disguise for the environment. And that's why the Nature Conservancy has chosen the Green River ecosystem as one of its prime spots to put a lot of effort into."

Working in partnership with the Nature Conservancy, the federal government's Green River Conservation Reserve Enhancement Program is paying Jimmy and other farmers along the river to take their land out of production and plant it instead in native grasses and trees. It's a good deal, says Jimmy, for farmers struggling to survive: "If farmers will set their land aside and apply the regulations of the program, they will be paid so much per acre per year for a period of time to be in that program. Quite frankly, it pays them more money than they can make raising cattle or corn or anything. Not quite as much as tobacco, but this is bottomland along the river, and you wouldn't plant tobacco there. That's been the main focus of the Nature Conservancy and the CREP program—if they can get the land along the Green River planted in timber and native grasses, that would protect the river from erosion and agricultural runoff and enhance the wildlife habitat, thereby improving the environment of the river. That's the goal. And it's been a very successful program, basically because they are paying farmers so much to be in the program that they cannot afford not to. So it's going really well. We've got bobwhites back at Apple Hill this year—first time I've heard them in five years. They're all on those grasses down along the river."

THE TIMBER

Although forestry is a major employer in Hart County today, Jimmy Middleton knows that "if we can improve the quality of our forest we can add a great deal to the economy of the county and, quite frankly, get this county back on its feet again." And that makes timber a major piece of the plan—the dollars-and-cents piece. He explains: "Hart County today is better than 50 percent forest. At one time, though, it was more than that. From the time the settlers first came here, they started cutting down trees. They would do it to clear a place to live on and to build their homes. Then over a long period of time the logging industry developed. Loggers would cut down trees for all kinds of uses. But there was no plan. They'd go out and cut the best trees—the most valuable ones. So over generations, they would cut the best and leave the worst, and the next generation would come along and take the best of what was left. Your woods were left with poorer-quality timber regenerating. Over time,

our forests were degraded, and today they are not nearly as valuable as they were years ago. If we could re-establish forests like they were then, we could start a chain reaction that would turn things around."

In addition to planting walnut trees in the bottoms, Jimmy plants red oaks on his land above the river—thousands of them, by hand, because he thinks his grandchildren's future, and the future of Hart County, lies in the forest. By his estimate, he has planted about 300,000 trees to date—and he plans to put in 450,000 more. That's three-quarters of a million trees. "They're four- to five-foot saplings, big enough to have a pretty good chance of getting established and getting above the other stuff that's growing in there—the competition." Those trees will mature in about seventy years, and although Jimmy won't be around to see them, he hopes some of his family will be. "I hope my grandchildren will be taking care of this land in the future—and maybe by that time, there'll be a good forest out there."

THE GRASSES

When the first Europeans came upon this region of Kentucky, they discovered an area very different from the rugged hills and thick forests to the east. Early documentation of south-central and western Kentucky describes vast plains of grasslands with trees widely scattered or absent. There are even legendary tales of people riding on horseback for days and at times not being able to see over the tops of the grasses. And while these days, if you drive south on Highway 31W you'll pass field after field of soybeans, 250 years ago this land was known as the Barrens.

"A Frenchman described this area in the late 1770s as an open plains area and talked about how the Indians burned it off to cultivate the buffalo—this was their hunting ground. The Buffalo Trace came right through here. The buffalo would cross the river, head north, and come up where town is today, right up Main Street, right where my clinic is. This was a huge open area, a semi-barren grassland. They'd come out in these barrens and graze and raise their calves. So to promote that, the Indians would burn it off every so often to keep it as grassland. And over hundreds of years, these native grasses adapted to that kind of environment—with the buffalo stomping all over the seed and scattering the seed—and they survived, and we ended up with a barren plains environment. That type of environment is much more conducive to wildlife," says the doctor, so he started planting some of his land above the river in grasses, too—land that once grew fescue and tobacco.

"We planted all this a few years ago, and the conservation people burned it off for the first time this year. That keeps it healthy. Come on out here," he says, lifting the barbed wire so you can shush through the tall grasses.

"See when you walk out in this stuff how different it is from fescue? See how there are animal tracks and trails in here? It's not thick underneath, and the little animals can hide in there and live in there, and the birds can run all through it. Over there in that fescue, they can't do that. And that's a big secret!" Jimmy estimates that half of his land is now in timber and the rest is open ground on which he raises cattle and fescue for sod, "which still makes fairly decent pasture."

THERE ARE EVEN LEGENDARY TALES OF PEOPLE RIDING ON HORSEBACK FOR DAYS AND AT TIMES NOT BEING ABLE TO SEE OVER THE TOPS OF THE GRASSES.

"I've got sixty acres in grasses up here," he says, " and we'll put in three hundred more next year. When you have this stuff, you get your rabbits back, and when you get your rabbits back, you get your hawks back; you get your bobcats back and your foxes. You get all the predators, and when that happens, the whole environment changes back again." Gesturing toward a pristine landscape that holds "tons of food and tons of protection," he says, "That's what this country looked like three hundred years ago, they claim. That's the real McCoy."

There's a fire in Jimmy Middleton born of understanding, and of his capacity to think in terms of three hundred years back and three hundred years into the future. So I asked him: What about the small farms?

"The small farms are gone. Farmers my age, their children have gone to work in the factory—it's a lot easier life. But all those guys still have that rural background. They still love the outdoors. They want to go turkey hunting and deer hunting. It's a big thing with them. And they will pay a landowner to use the land for hunting—to have a cabin in the woods, to have a place.

" A FRENCHMAN DESCRIBED THIS AREA IN THE LATE 1770'S AS AN OPEN
PLAINS AREA AND TALKED ABOUT HOW THE INDIANS BURNED IT OFF TO CULTIVATE
THE BUFFALO - THIS WAS THEIR HUNTING GROUND.

THE BUFFALO TRACE CAME RIGHT THROUGH HERE. THE BUFFALO WOULD
CROSS THE RIVER, HEAD NORTH, AND COME UP WHERE THE TOWN IS TODAY,
RIGHT UP MAIN STREET, RIGHT WHERE MY CLINIC IS. **"**

—Jimmy Middleton

Apple by Roger Blair

“ I LOVE HOLDING LAND

AND WORKING WITH LAND,

AND I THINK THAT'S WHAT

MY FAMILY WILL BE DOING—

GROWING TIMBER AND

LEASING OUT LAND FOR

HUNTING AND RECREATION.

AND IN THE FUTURE,

IF YOU KEEP IT UP RIGHT,

YOU'RE REALLY GONNA

HAVE SOMETHING. ”

—Jimmy Middleton

MOVING MOUNTAINS

Daymon Morgan lives at the edge of a lush one hundred-acre forest in Leslie County, deep in the coalfield region of the Appalachian Mountains of Eastern Kentucky. He knows every tree and herb in these mountains and has at times supplemented his income by collecting and selling medicinal organic herbs and by selective logging.

Daymon was born not far from where he and his wife, Betty, live today in a rustic and pleasant log home at the end of a seven-mile stretch of steep mountain road called Lower Bad Creek. They are one of only five families on the mountain. "My daddy laid these logs when I was eleven years old," Daymon says as he comes down the steps to meet me.

Stewardship

| LOWER BAD CREEK |

{ | DAYMON MORGAN | }

7

Daymon Morgan is a World War II vet in his early eighties, handsome, with white hair, blue eyes, and large hands. He's dressed in overalls and moves with the agility of a much younger man. He seems gregarious and easy, used to making strangers feel at home, and he probably most often looks on the bright side of things. Yet, for most of his life he has been fighting for the right of the people of these mountains to hold on to their heritage, and considering all he's seen, it's a wonder Daymon Morgan has any spirit left.

Daymon has been a member of an organization called Kentuckians for the Commonwealth (KFTC), the state's largest social justice organization, since its inception in 1981 and has also served as its chairman. Among other things, KFTC, with its five-thousand-plus members, helps coalfield residents fight corporations that have turned so much of Eastern Kentucky into what some have called a toxic dump. He also did a stint as chairman of the Citizen's Coal Council, a national organization made up of people who live in coal-mining or coal-impacted states.

As a member of KFTC, Daymon has taken hundreds of people on tours of his property, speaking to them about his love and concern for the mountainous land above Lower Bad Creek, land he has nurtured and defended for fifty years. Daymon enjoys people, and he knows about mining.

 I TAKE PEOPLE ON TOURS UP HERE," HE SAYS, "TO SHOW THEM WHAT'S GOING ON.

What's "going on" is that over the past 130 years the coal industry has removed more than 9 billion tons of coal from Kentucky. And now, with the advent of a particularly destructive method of strip mining known as mountaintop removal, it takes no more than ten men and a couple of mammoth machines—big as buildings and operating around the clock—to blast off the top of a mountain, dump it in the valley below, and rake out the coal. And the mountain is gone for good. This is what's happening in Central Appalachia, and the forests—which are the oldest and most diverse in North America—are disappearing at an alarming rate, along with clean air and water, clear streams, wildlife, jobs, homes, and hope. And somewhere in the midst of all this is Daymon Morgan and his hundred-acre forest.

We climb into his Argo, a six-wheel amphibious ATV, and head for his forest. The little vehicle will go four miles per hour over land or water. It's warm for November, and rain is on the way. As we head up the narrow rock road, his voice rises above the grating of the engine, and he tells of hunting deer, rabbit, wild turkey, and squirrel. He points out a Russian olive tree and tells of making jelly from its berries, and berry pie.

" WHAT'S 'GOING ON' IS THAT OVER THE PAST 130 YEARS
THE COAL INDUSTRY HAS REMOVED MORE THAN 9 BILLION TONS OF
COAL FROM KENTUCKY. AND NOW, WITH THE ADVENT OF A PARTICULARLY
DESTRUCTIVE METHOD OF STRIP MINING KNOWN AS

MOUNTAINTOP REMOVAL, IT TAKES NO MORE THAN TEN MEN AND A
COUPLE OF MAMMOTH MACHINES—BIG AS BUILDINGS AND OPERATING AROUND
THE CLOCK—TO BLAST OFF THE TOP OF A MOUNTAIN,
DUMP IT IN THE VALLEY BELOW, AND RAKE OUT THE COAL. ,,

"I grew up back across the mountain in Camp Creek, in my daddy's house. I was the oldest. Had eleven brothers and sisters. When we were old enough to carry a hoe we had to work the farm. That's the way we made a living. We'd clear out the hillside and plant corn and beans. Soil was so rich we didn't need fertilizer. We had hogs, too, and we'd turn 'em loose all up in here and they'd eat beechnuts all summer long."

These are proud people, these mountain people. The mountains have shaped their culture and defined their heritage over generations. They are endowed with the deep traditions of a culture every bit as rich as that of the American Indian. They are independent and free-thinking, storytellers and musicians, reared to take care of themselves and live from the land. And although work was hard, farming, hunting, and gathering herbs sustained families like Daymon's—until the railroads came along and that changed everything. The timber barons came first, and when they left they took most of the beech trees with them.

Daymon points out the tree where the wild bees live, and wild ginger. "I cook with it, make medicine, tea. I was raised where there weren't any doctors. My grandparents and parents passed down the old remedies."

I ask what he uses from these woods to make his medicine. "Well, I use that wild ginger and goldenseal, and then I use that cherry birch bark and red sassafras and pokeberry and garlic and apple cider vinegar. That's pure apple cider vinegar—not filtered!"

"You don't mix them all together, do you?" I ask.

"Yep," he chuckles. "I make about two gallons at a time. I've got a little two-ounce cup, and every morning I take a little of that. I don't drink it for the taste, now—it doesn't taste too good. But it's a good tonic. Good for your blood, good for your stomach, good for everything."

We're about halfway up the mountain and looking down into a deep-valley forest where a small stream pushes its way through the vegetation.

"I'd walk through here and hunt as a kid, fish in that creek down there. Hunted ginseng. Then while I was in the army I thought a lot about this place. So when I got out, I bought it. A hundred acres."

Today, Daymon Morgan's hundred-acre forest is the only stretch along Lower Bad Creek that hasn't been strip-mined.

"There was no road here then. Only way you could get to it was to walk down the creek bed." He points out the cottage where he lived by himself; only the crumbled chimney is left. "When I bought that place, an old man and woman lived there. That old man was a real mountain man—big man, and he'd go barefoot in the wintertime. He made moonshine whiskey back up on top of that mountain. He had a dinner bell down there, and if anybody'd come around that was strange, his wife would go out there and tap that bell, and he'd run off from that still."

He stops at a spindly tree, an American chestnut, with a red ribbon tied around its trunk. "Years before my time, there were chestnut trees all over these woods, all through the Appalachians. People would go out in wintertime and pick 'em up and eat 'em. They were real good. Hogs would eat 'em, turkeys, everything. But back about one hundred years ago a blight came through here and killed all of them. Now there's a place in Virginia that's tryin' to get 'em started again. They've got a test farm over there to try and get that blight out of 'em. I heard about it, and I ordered fifty of those trees a few years ago. They were just little bitty things. Here's one of 'em—it's grown a lot."

I'm noticing that Daymon talks of these trees and herbs in his forest as if they were his children. Daymon's children are gone—all seven of them. Moved on to other opportunities, like most of the children of these mountains.

He leans down and scoops away some rotting leaves and brings up a huge handful of soil that is so black and rich it looks like velvet.

"This kind of soil—you won't find it after they strip mine. See that," he says, holding it up close to me, and his voice takes on a frustration that I'm beginning to understand. "All this here is certified organic. This is hundreds and hundreds of years of leaves. It's natural. It's not contaminated. There's no chemicals in it.

Herbs—not too long ago they were everywhere in these mountains. Before the bulldozers and explosives came. Like many people, I have read about mountaintop removal—seen pictures—but I've never heard anyone explain how we came to this better than Daymon Morgan.

BLOODROOT

MAYAPPLE

AMERICAN CHESTNUT

MAYAPPLE

"If you've got herbs growing on certified organic land and you want to sell 'em, they're worth a lot of money. I dug ginseng way back when I was growin' up. It was eight dollars a pound then. I've still got some, but it's pretty scarce. We've had a lot of poachers, you see. Price is about six hundred dollars now. Everybody's lookin' for it."

Herbs—not too long ago they were everywhere in these mountains. Before the bulldozers and explosives came. Like many people, I have read about mountaintop removal—seen pictures—but I've never heard anyone explain how we came to this better than Daymon Morgan.

"Years ago, around the turn of the century, there were speculators coming through here—and big companies, too—buying up mineral rights for as little as twenty-five cents an acre. The farmers didn't sell their surface land, because they could farm it to make a living. Most of the people that lived here at that time, they couldn't imagine a time when coal would be worth anything, so they sold their mineral rights. And a quarter an acre—that was a little money for 'em. The companies took advantage of them. They were uneducated, and they signed that contract.

"Back then there was no way that coal mining could do much damage to the land. There were no coal trucks, no bulldozers, no high explosives, so really, miners pulled that coal out of the mountain with little small ponies. And these people could not foresee in the future that coal would be worth a lot, so they sold it. Of course, over the years, they had the same old deed, and it was handed down to different people when they died. But with the modern methods of mining they got now, using the language from back one hundred years—those coal companies, they'd come in and tear your land apart and there wasn't a thing you could do about it. So we finally got a law passed in 1988 by a constitutional amendment, voted on by the people of Kentucky. We beat them four to one, and since then, the coal companies have not had that right to go in and tear up your land and get that coal without your permission."

It was a huge victory, but the reality was, a major portion of the land was already controlled by outside corporations—profit was the bottom line—and the amendment could not end the impact of strip mining on land adjacent to vast holdings owned or leased by those companies. By early in the new millennium nearly five hundred mountains had been cut down. And the amount of stripped acreage continues to grow—jobs are few in the region, and coal companies pay well for permission.

When I ask Daymon if he thinks he'll see the end of all of this, he is silent. "Well," he says with a little hop and a whole new burst of energy as he ushers me back into the Argo, "now, I'll take you up there and show you a little bit of first-class destruction."

Farther up the mountain, we chug to a stop and climb the steep embankment to the top of the ridge. "I own everything from here back down to my cabin," Daymon says. "And this, everything over here—at least, the mineral rights—belongs to the coal companies."

In front of us, the beautiful forest drops off literally into a site being excavated before our eyes, a vast and lifeless landscape, a wasteland drained of all color and stretching as far as the eye can see. The sight is horrific and gut wrenching.

"Do you know the person who owns this land?" I ask.

"The man who owns this, he has all kinds of money. He's almost ninety years old—got more money than he can spend in a lifetime."

We stand there for a while, silent. There is nothing to say. After that, we climb back into the Argo and head for a different vista, a mine site reclaimed more than thirty years ago which abuts his land and is typical, with its few pines and black locusts struggling to grow in the crushed shale. We're making our way at four miles per hour across what looks like the surface of the moon. There's gravel, dry dirt, potholes, and, remarkably, cattle and horses grazing on sparse tall grasses and broom sage. "This land belongs to one of the coal companies, and they don't care if farmers' livestock graze there. It's good advertising for them. Makes it look like the land is good for something—which it isn't." Daymon does say, however, that the coal companies are beginning to do a little better—planting lespedeza and sweet clover. "The land will grow certain things, but it'll never get back where it was."

"What shall we say to our children and grandchildren when they see hundreds of miles of bereft, tabletop mountains, which will be the heritage of Eastern Kentucky? Will it be sufficient to say, 'We needed the coal so we destroyed the mountains and the people?'"

—Barry Bingham, Jr,
2005

Coal companies will tell you that it's beautiful on top of these mountains after a mined area has been restored and turned into grazing land for cattle, horses, elk, and deer. But they're wrong. You can make level land, but you can't grow anything decent on it. The topsoil is gone. And scientists say that it will take at least a thousand years to build it back. Coal officials will also tell you that mountaintop mining is good for Appalachia, that it produces jobs, much-needed flat land, and opportunities for its people. But the fact is that over the past two decades coal employment in Kentucky has dropped by almost two-thirds. It doesn't take too many people to run the big machines. And to the argument that mountaintop strip mining is necessary for the sake of low-cost coal, Wendell Berry responds in an article that appeared in the *Courier-Journal*: "We have 'low-cost coal' only because the real cost of such mining is charged to the citizens and residents of the coalfields, to the forest ecosystems and watersheds of the Cumberland Plateau, to all of us who live downstream, and to everybody's children."

We stop one last time, and Daymon points out what used to be Huckleberry Ridge, where he picked huckleberries as a child. The huge mountain that was Huckleberry Ridge is gone. "At one time there were mountains all through here—high mountains and timber. Why, this was the finest timber you could find. They took it, and what they didn't take they shoved over the edge. I tell you what I've done. I've taken people up here who have never been in the state of Kentucky before—from New York and all. They look at stuff like that and stand there an' cry."

We head back down the mountain, back into the shelter of his forest. I don't know what to say. The law that Daymon Morgan fought so hard to pass twenty years ago saved his home and land, but every day he has to look out at thousands of acres destroyed in every direction.

"Sometime back, a coal company engineer came in here and said if I'd let them mine this land here above the road—not down the hill there— they'd build me a big fish pond down there and put in a good road across it and make me some level land. I said no way."

"What do you think you'd tell him if he came back?" I ask.

"I don't know. He estimated that I had a million ton of coal on that side, and I think they pay about two dollars a ton—for tearing your land up. I for sure won't lease 'em anything below the road. Up there on top of the hill though, I don't know. There's no herbs on it, timber's no good. Just a real dry mountain. But it's got big veins of coal under it. They want to lease the land, take the coal out of it. They told me they'd put it back, sow it, put me any kind of pasture I wanted, put me some level land up there, build me a big fish pond, build me a good road across it, and pay me about two dollars a ton. What would you do?"

In 2005, the late Barry Bingham Jr., who was editor and publisher of the *Courier-Journal* from 1971 to 1986, wrote an article about mountaintop removal in which he observed that the topography of Eastern Kentucky is very similar to the mountains of Tennessee and North Carolina, which he had visited with his family on a trip to the Smoky Mountains National Park. "The fact that the Smoky Mountains is the most visited park in the United States… sends us a clear message: The people of this country are attracted by beauty and nature in its pristine state. What shall we say to our children and grandchildren when they see hundreds of miles of bereft, tabletop mountains, which will be the heritage of Eastern Kentucky? Will it be sufficient to say, 'We needed the coal so we destroyed the mountains and the people?' "

I phoned Daymon Morgan several months after my visit and asked him how things were going over there. At the time the Obama administration had taken tough steps to restrict the pollution of streams from new mountaintop coal mining projects and hopefully, this time it was going to make a difference. Daymon was his usual cheerful, optimistic self as he briefed me on his hundred-acre forest. He said his little chestnut trees—the ones in the sun, anyway—were thirty feet high.

GOOD GRIEF

"We buried the state of Kentucky once in a pine box. We were protesting out-of-state garbage coming in; they wanted to make this a big landfill and let people from all over the place come in here and dump their trash, dump their garbage. So we were protesting that, and we went down there to Frankfort and we buried the state of Kentucky in a pine box. We met up about twenty miles outside of Frankfort and had the funeral procession. We had a police escort right over to the Capitol Building, and we got to the rotunda there, and that's where we had the funeral service. The pastor preached about Kentucky being admitted to the union, and how it suffered all the abuse from the coal companies and big timber companies and finally died of an overdose of out-of-state garbage. We had graveside services behind the Capitol. I think Wallace Wilkinson was governor. We took the death certificate and laid it up there on the governor's desk. 'Course, he wasn't there. Said he regretted he couldn't be here today."

—Daymon Morgan

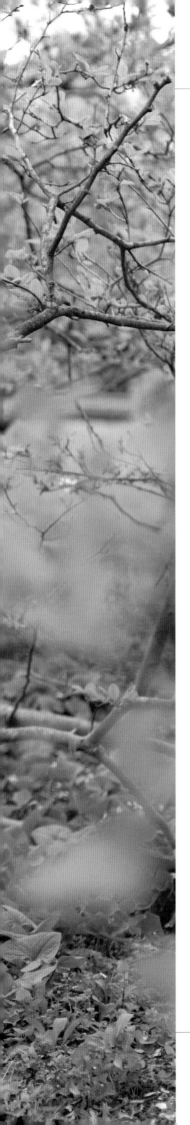

SAVOIR-FAIRE

Kentucky's brand of hospitality is unrivaled. It is what gives pause to first-time visitors and finds them longing to return again and again. It has a warmth and genuineness that has been handed down from generation to generation, like a family heirloom.

Even in such a context, Kathy Cary's Louisville restaurant is special. Known as one of the finest restaurants in the southeast, Lilly's features locally raised products and is on every gourmet's list of places to eat in Kentucky. But the thing that becomes crystal-clear to those meeting the blond, blue-eyed chef for the first time is that her restaurant is a direct reflection of her personality: warm, energetic, friendly, and elegant. It feels like home.

Hospitality

| LILLY'S RESTAURANT |

{ | KATHY NASH CARY |

| LONGFIELD FARM |

8

In 1993, seven years after opening Lilly's, Kathy became the first Kentucky chef to cook at the James Beard House in New York. That night, she and her staff served a six-course dinner for one hundred people, starting with Kentucky country ham with bleu cheese and chives and ending with Shaker lemon tart. They brought pieces of Kentucky limestone to decorate the hors d'oeuvre trays. They made yeast rolls.

"A few minutes before the guests arrived," Kathy remembers, "we snaked through the house with those rolls, and it smelled fabulous."

Kathy's sense of what it takes to make people feel special and cared for is born of her Kentucky roots. Her parents, Sissy and Bobby Nash, had a passion for riding and wanted to raise their three girls in the country, so they bought a farm, and because it felt so far from civilization, they named it Longfield for Sissy's grandfather's farm in Ireland. Like so much of Kentucky's landscape, Longfield has rolling fields and fence lines, grazing cattle and horse barns, orchards and hay bales and gardens lovingly tended. But along with all of that, Longfield is a place of hospitality.

"It was paradise," Kathy recalls. "Back then people thought we lived way out in the middle of nowhere. We'd have friends come home with us from school on Friday, and their parents wouldn't pick them up until Sunday because we were soooo far out."

Kathy's world was three hundred acres of horseback riding, ice skating on frozen creeks, playing cowboys and Indians—and miles and miles of freedom. "That farm raised me," she says.

"The rule was no TV. We were outside the entire day, exploring, riding, jumping on the back of the hay wagon. No one said, 'Where are you going? What time will you be back?' There were no cell phones."

> KATHY'S WORLD WAS THREE HUNDRED ACRES OF HORSEBACK RIDING, ICE SKATING ON FROZEN CREEKS, PLAYING COWBOYS AND INDIANS—AND MILES AND MILES OF FREEDOM. 'THAT FARM RAISED ME,' SHE SAYS.

—Kathy Cary

Bobby Nash worked in the city in the family's bourbon business, coming home every evening to the country life. Although he kept foxhounds down the road and polo ponies in the stables, Longfield was a real working farm that raised Black Angus cattle, corn, and hay, and Kathy and her sisters were expected to pull their own weight. Their father taught them about love and respect for the land, and about the importance of community.

"On Sundays," says Kathy, "we didn't have a choice. After church and a big sit-down lunch we'd go on a rough-ride with Daddy—two or three hours. We'd blaze trails in the rain, sleet, snow. 'Girls, lets go,' he'd say. We'd blaze and clear not only on our own property but the neighbors' too."

Kathy's mother, Sissy, is soft-spoken but wildly creative, and her Irish genes are evident when she describes the moment she fell in love with what was to be the family's new home.

"What really won me over was coming down the stairs into the front hall. The banister was so wide, it felt like the kind you could swing a leg over and slide down. It was just so hospitable."

Sunday lunch was always a family affair, often at Sissy's mother's house "in town," where young Kathy would head for the kitchen to watch Lyda Newton, who cooked for her grandmother.

"Kathy," her mother remembers, "was quite little when she started liking to be in the kitchen. I would hoist her up on my hip to watch me make hollandaise sauce. She'd say, 'Show me what you do.' "

As time went on, ambiance became important.

"One night we had friends over for supper. The twins had gone out and Kathy said she'd fix her own. We were on the terrace when one of our guests came out of the house and said, 'Someone is sitting at the little table in the dining room with a lace mat in front of them and a candle lit.' I said, 'That's Kathy.' That was just the way she was."

An evening at Longfield in fine weather meant a walk in Sissy Nash's famous gardens, great conversation, fabulous food, and adventure.

"Our Impressionist parties were my favorite," Sissy remembers. "People would come dressed as someone from the nineteenth century. We had planted a wildflower meadow at the top of the hill. We'd have a little string quartet playing Baroque music and Gypsy music down by the house. It was fun because people would enjoy the flowers in the garden and the music and not really see the wildflowers and the tables all set up until they got to the top of the hill."

There were garden parties, polo parties, family weddings, wedding parties for children of friends, and of course, the annual Derby brunch—because, as Sissy says, "part of the fun of having a place is sharing it."

For Kathy, those parties meant getting to spend time with the women who cooked in her mother's kitchen. "Sometimes Sarah Howard would come to help, and I would hang out in the kitchen with her. I learned how to make Sarah Howard's lemon squares. They were perfect."

She was inspired, she says, by the women who cooked for her mother and grandmother.

 THEY WERE FABULOUS COOKS.
I WAS FASCINATED WATCHING THEM.
NO RECIPES, NO BOOKS, JUST MEMORY
AND TASTE AND FEEL. THE SIMPLICITY
OF IT! I FIRMLY BELIEVE THAT
I LEARNED TO COOK FROM EXPERTS
WITH NO CULINARY DEGREE.

—Kathy Cary

"

AS I GOT OLDER, I'D GO
DOWN TO THE VEGETABLE
GARDEN, AND I BEGAN
TO REALIZE THAT
WAS DINNER—
THAT WAS A MEAL—
AND BY JUST PICKING
THE RIGHT THINGS,
I COULD FEED PEOPLE!

—Kathy Cary

"

Today at Longfield, it's the grounds and renowned flower gardens that get most of the attention, but when Kathy and her sisters were growing up, "Mother was more interested in vegetables—and the vegetable garden was huge. We had apples, cherries, beans, and tomatoes, so many that we had to can them. And we helped with that. We had to. It was part of the deal. Later on, as we started dating, we'd say, 'I'm going out tonight,' and my parents would say, 'Not until you've picked five pints of strawberries.' Or if a cow had just been killed, we'd have to sit there and make five hundred meat patties—that's one cow. Then we could go out.

"As I got older, I'd go down to the vegetable garden, and I began to realize that was dinner—that was a meal—and by just picking the right things, I could feed people! So I started entertaining my friends from school. I was about fifteen, and I thought it was fun to show them that I could fix a meal without ever leaving the farm. And that was the beginning of my cooking career, I would say."

Just out of high school, the independent young Kathy moved to Washington, D.C. Instead of college, she went to cooking school, apprenticed to a Cordon Bleu–trained chef, and started a small catering firm that did parties "for some pretty high-end clients."

"Then, while I was home one summer, I met Will Cary. That was it. I knew him for a week and moved back to Louisville." She married the singer-songwriter and in 1978 opened her first hometown business, La Peche Gourmet to Go.

Ten years later, Kathy and Will opened their restaurant in a one hundred-year-old building in the historic Highlands neighborhood of Louisville and named it for their daughter, Lilly. It was a time when there were few restaurants in the city, and a time when only a few people—worried about what industrial food production was doing to the land, rural communities, and the family farm—were talking about something called "sustainable agriculture."

> " WHEN WE OPENED, THERE WERE NO FARMS WHERE WE COULD GO TO GET PRODUCE. I WOULD GO OUT TO MY PARENTS' FARM ON SUNDAY AND PICK WATERCRESS OUT OF THE CREEK TO HAVE ON THE MENU FOR THE COMING WEEK. "
>
> —Kathy Cary

"And then one day, Bruce showed up at our door." Bruce (who uses no last name) and his partner, Carol Friedman, had an organic farm an hour south of Louisville, in Hart County. "They grew the most beautiful vegetables I'd ever seen—baby bok choy and snow peapod tendrils. They started bringing their truck up every Thursday, and I'd buy everything they had. Literally."

It was the early nineties, and things were beginning to change. Slowly, other farmers started showing up at Lilly's and other small independent restaurants around town, asking, "Would you want to buy a few tomatoes?"

Wanting to buy more local produce and realizing that other chefs might as well, Kathy organized a meeting on a Monday morning at Lilly's. "We had chefs, farmers, and food writers, as well as some people from the State Agricultural Department in Frankfort. We all sat down together and talked about what was going on and what we could do. We were tired of some of our regular produce suppliers—bringing stuff that wasn't nearly as high quality as what we could get here, from our farmers. It was coming mostly from California, and we felt there was a real need here to change tactics, for a lot of reasons.

The farmers wanted to sell to us direct, with no middleman. They wanted to call us on the phone, tell us what they had, see what we wanted and when we wanted delivery. Two or three of us started doing it. It was more homework for us, more phone calls, but the quality was there, the farmer got cash or a check immediately, and we built a healthy relationship with them. It was simple and honest, a handshake.

I was able to say, 'I'm doing a wedding in three months, and I need to make eggplant Parmesan for four hundred. Please, can you?' 'Yes, I can.' 'Great.' And then they started calling us in winter saying, 'What would you like us to plant for next year?' All of that has worked into a great relationship.

"When you look at packaged vegetables in some grocery stores, a lot of them are color enhanced and polished, and they don't taste all that good. They've been trucked in from a long way away, and they're not helping the farmer down the road who's growing the good-tasting carrots and the blue Cinderella pumpkins. Each farmer is a story, and you can put really pretty names on the menu, like 'Cinderella Pumpkin Soup.' How pretty is that? 'Cinderella pumpkins grown by Ivor Chodkowski.'"

Handpicking only the best, building dishes and menus around locally grown products, and naming dishes on her menu for the people who produced their ingredients have become Kathy's stock-in-trade. She has been written about in most of the country's leading food publications, has made network TV appearances, and has been back to cook at the James Beard House five times. She is one of those responsible for putting Kentucky—long known for its wonderful produce but not for its cuisine—in the national culinary spotlight.

Behind her success is something very basic: the strong work ethic that came with the family genes. "My father said I'm blessed and cursed by it," she recalls laughing, "and I said, 'I know it!' "

BEHIND HER SUCCESS IS SOMETHING VERY BASIC:
THE STRONG WORK ETHIC THAT CAME WITH THE FAMILY GENES.
"MY FATHER SAID I'M BLESSED AND CURSED BY IT,"
SHE RECALLS, LAUGHING, "AND I SAID, 'I KNOW IT!'"

—Kathy Cary

TANYA, VIRGINIA, KATIE AND MARY BERRY SMITH

A VINEYARD VANTAGE POINT

When Mary Berry was little she spent a lot of time at her grandparents' big white house in town. "It was a magical place," she says, "a place where time slowed down—and when my grandparents died I thought I was going to die if that house was sold." But it wasn't. When Mary's in-laws sold their dairy farm, they bought the house. And someday, says Mary, "one of our daughters will live there. I'm so happy about that."

Things seem to work that way for this family—staying in one place. It's in the genes.

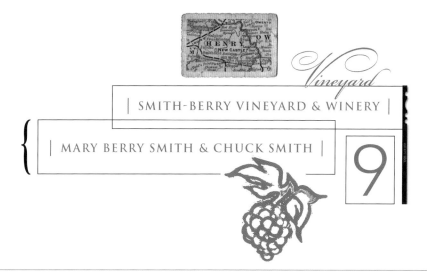

| SMITH-BERRY VINEYARD & WINERY |

{ | MARY BERRY SMITH & CHUCK SMITH |

9

> " I GREW UP WITH NO TV. I USED TO THINK IF SOMEBODY HAD A TV AND A RANCH HOUSE, THEY WERE FABULOUSLY WEALTHY. "
>
> — Mary Berry Smith

Mary and her husband, Chuck Smith, are eighth-generation farmers. "We bought this farm when we were married," says Mary. "We were both twenty-two, and my grandfather said, 'You'll never pay for it.'" The farm consists of 180 acres near the small town of New Castle, on the northern edge of the Bluegrass. Until recently, Mary and Chuck made a go of it by growing tobacco and raising dairy cattle. They also raised vegetables and pastured poultry, which they sold at farmers' markets as well as to customers who enjoyed the trek to the country to buy from this farming family. Over time those relationships grew.

"I grew up with no TV," Mary recalls. "I used to think if somebody had a TV and a ranch house, they were fabulously wealthy. Our girls—growing up here, working here—they understood what money meant. When they wanted a CD or something, they'd say, 'That's half a bushel of tomatoes.' They knew how many chickens that would be."

With everybody pitching in, the family processed three thousand chickens a season, but finding good labor was a problem. "You couldn't just hire anyone. Our kids were great at it, but you can't keep your children home from college to kill chickens," says Mary, who gets her point across with few words and dry wit.

"Chuck and I realized, though, that we were not getting ahead. We were wearing ourselves out, along with the land." They swapped the dairy cattle for beef and, over three years, became organic while continuing to raise tobacco and pastured poultry. That model worked for a while, but the handwriting was on the wall.

"We knew by the late eighties that tobacco would not survive," Mary says. She and Chuck began to consider how they might leave their children with a viable operation, should they choose to carry on the family's farming tradition.

Then, in 1996, while vacationing in northern California, Chuck got into a conversation with a vineyard owner. "How many acres of grapes do you have?" he asked.

"Eight," replied the vintner.

"That's tobacco," Chuck exclaimed—and with that, the Smiths had happened upon an agricultural product that would work well in Kentucky, with its climate and soil not so different from the wine-growing regions of France. (In fact, Kentucky was one of the biggest wine-producing states in the country before prohibition.)

"For a long time," Mary explains, "people on marginal farms such as ours have made a living on small acreage of a cash crop like tobacco. So from that moment on we researched wine. Chuck did an internship at Fetzer. He lobbied the legislature to pass the Farm Winery Act, which would allow people like us in dry counties to have a local option election and be able to sell wine. And it passed."

Grapes are an expensive endeavor and, like tobacco, largely dependent on crop yield for profit. Unlike tobacco, which is planted and harvested annually, grapes take several years before the first crop is ready to be turned into wine. But Chuck Smith figured that, acre for acre, grapes would yield at least as much profit as tobacco.

Over six years the Smiths studied, worked on legislation, and prepared for what lay ahead. They received some money from the tobacco settlement and generated a bit more through a grant. "With those funds," says Mary, "we were able to work on the winery and the tasting room and the old tobacco barn, where we now have concerts. They are all structures that were here originally."

When Smith-Berry Winery opened in the summer of 2002—the same summer the family pulled in their last crop of tobacco—the old dairy had been turned into an art gallery, its walls hung with a stunning collection of black-and-white photographs

by James Baker Hall. The exhibit was titled "Tobacco Harvest: An Elegy."

"It was a homecoming, a fulfillment of sort," wrote Mary's father, Wendell Berry, in an essay for the book that accompanied the exhibit. "A lot of people came to see the pictures, on opening day and on other days. Old tobacco men stood looking at them and wept. It was as though, across a long interval of time, a window had been opened through which we saw ourselves as we once were. And we were grateful for this witness to the light we had."

It was the beginning of a new era, and the people kept coming. Today, Mary and Chuck raise organic beef cattle, sheep, hay, organic vegetables, and of course, grapes. With the help of their three daughters—Katie, Virginia, and Tanya—they take those grapes from the vine to the bottle. Each weekend, the Smiths and the tobacco barn play host to a concert and cookout that draws hundreds. It's a family effort that requires days of preparation. "The girls do whatever is needed at the time," says Mary. Tanya is not quite twenty-one and can't sell wine yet, so she parks cars. Chuck grills chicken, hamburgers, and corn on the mammoth grills, helped by whomever is available. Sometimes that's Mary's brother, Den Berry, who is a carrier of the family sense of humor as well. "They turned me loose with the salt shaker a while back," Den recalls, "and I went a little far, but Chuck said it was okay—they sold a lot of wine."

The rest of the cooking takes place in the tiny kitchen of the tasting room. "Most of the vegetables we use are grown here," says Mary, "but what we don't raise we buy from other farmers close by. The thing I love about the concerts is that not only do we get people from the region, it's a social gathering for the community."

It's family—you can feel it.

"A lot of people came to see the pictures, on opening day and on other days. Old tobacco men stood looking at them and wept. It was as though, across a long interval of time, a window had been opened through which we saw ourselves as we once were. And we were grateful for this witness to the light we had."

— Wendell Berry
Tobacco Harvest: An Elegy

TOBACCO HARVEST,
Photo by James Baker Hall, 1973
Courtesy of The James Baker Hall Archive

People arrive early toting lawn chairs and picnic blankets. They sit listening to the bluegrass band and sipping glasses of wine made right on the property. Many are the same customers that years ago made the drive to the country to buy vegetables and chicken. "They are not just our customers," Mary says. "They are friends." The backdrop is kids frolicking on hay bales—climbing up, jumping off—and five and a half acres of three kinds of grapes: Chambourcin, Norton, and Vidal Blanc. The vineyard produces nineteen kinds of wine, which are sold in wine shops and to restaurants, as well as through direct sales and during all events at Smith-Berry Winery.

"Sometimes, when I'm going from one thing to the next—you know, there's always so much to do—I don't notice the beauty," says Mary. "But then I look around. What we have here is beautiful—beautiful buildings, beautiful land.

"When we bought this farm I was worried about paying for it. My dad said, 'If you take care of the nature on that place, the place will take care of you.' "

"And?" I ask.

"This year, sales are up 40 percent. Knock on wood."

JESSIE GRAY AND LONNIE ROBINSON

A Lost Art

In the southwest corner of Spain, about fifty miles from the Portuguese border, is the small and ancient town of Aracena. This is where, every other year, the World Ham Congress convenes, drawing together a small group of artisans recognized for producing the finest cured hams in the world. In 2009, the World Ham Congress extended its first invitation to a non-European producer: Nancy Newsom Mahaffey of Princeton, Kentucky, the smallest ham producer in the United States.

"It was such a wonderful honor for me," says Nancy. "In Spain, jamón is a tradition. In some areas it's more than that—it's a way of life."

Artisan

| NEWSOM'S COUNTRY HAMS |

{ | NANCY NEWSOM MAHAFFEY |

10

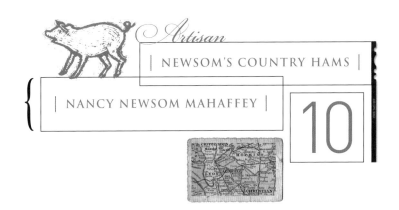

Ham has been a tradition in the Newsom family since the 1700s, when they came to Kentucky from Virginia, bringing with them the curing process, gleaned from a family will.

Nancy Newsom Mahaffey has been running the family business since 1987, when her father, Kentucky Colonel Bill Newsom, retired. "My granddaddy started the business in 1917," she says. "It was the only general store in the area, and he sold everything."

H.C. Newsom carried glassware and pickles; crackers and meat; garden seed, fresh cream, and goldfish. He cured hams for his family, but there was no market for them in his store. Back then, everybody cured hams. H. C. died in 1933, and Nancy's dad took over; he was just eighteen at the time. Bill Newsom and his wife eventually turned the store into a full-scale grocery and began curing hams for limited sale.

"By the 1950s and 1960s," says Nancy, "my father's hams were becoming well-known both in this area and by folks from other states who stopped by the store." In time, many ham producers switched to the quick-cure method, but Colonel Newsom stayed with the old way. At some point, Nancy says, her father perfected the process laid out in the old will, and since then, "it has never changed."

A Newsom ham is cured with only salt, sugar, and hickory smoke. No nitrites—and no nitrates, which are used in commercial curing to speed up the process. "When you don't use nitrates you end up with more of a hand-crafted product, because you have to rub that salt into the ham a whole lot longer. It takes a lot more time.

"I think one reason more and more people are liking the kinds of food that take a long time to produce—the 'slow food' kind of food—is that the world is moving ninety miles an hour. History in a business is important. All across America there's a growing feeling that it's good to be able to know where your food came from—and know the person that made it."

In 1975, James Beard discovered Bill Newsom's hams, and through Beard's syndicated column, Newsom's hams became known around the world. "After that," says Nancy, "other writers, newspapers, and magazines jumped on board to spread the word, and they continue to this day to do so, thank God."

Bill Newsom figured Nancy's older brother would run the business someday. "Dad wanted me to be a secretary," she says. But Nancy began taking care of mail orders in her early twenties, "and by twenty-six, I was working in the ham house with the men." She paid attention to the proportions of brown sugar and salt. "I watched Daddy over his shoulder. Well, I figured somebody had to know how to do it—just in case."

Then, in 1987, a massive fire destroyed the grocery. "Dad didn't want to stay in business, but I knew we had to, because the ham house was full of hams that weren't sold yet. I was out of work one day—I just couldn't stand it."

Nancy hastily set up shop in a former garden store two doors away from the grocery, "so I could ship my hams out. I thought we'd sell those hams and close up.

"The funny thing was, I put two mums up there at the site of the fire as a memorial, and before I could get halfway down the street somebody pulled up and wanted to buy them; and I put two more up there, and somebody wanted to buy them. And I said okay. I don't believe in coincidence. It was a sign. People kept coming in, paying their accounts. We didn't even know how much they owed, but they did. When January came it just felt natural to put hams in salt."

The building that today houses Newsom's Old Mill Store dates from the 1850s. In the early days, Civil War uniforms were produced there, and later, the Red Rose Flour Mill turned out one hundred barrels of flour a day. "Upstairs are two floors of 1892 flour mill equipment, which will be a museum someday," says Nancy.

Sweet Corn

How Sweet It Is

17 95 #

Some Sweet Corn

795 & up

14 95 #

BT Sweet Corn Peaches & Cream

Sweet Corn

Incredible

14 95 #

7 95 CUP

Sweet Corn
Ambrosia

3 ¼# AMBROSIA
Sweet
Co

Yellow
Corn sweet
FunKS
G 90

FUNK
G 90
Sweet Corn

SWEET CORN

SILVER KIN

SWEET CORN

SILVER KIN
Burton
Bros
Seed

GOLDEN C
Burton
Bros
Seed

Price

IN 1975, JAMES BEARD DISCOVERED BILL NEWSOM'S HAMS, AND THROUGH BEARD'S SYNDICATED COLUMN, NEWSOM'S HAMS BECAME KNOWN AROUND THE WORLD.

The market has grown to include a big Internet and mail-order business that ships hundreds of gourmet gift baskets for all occasions, especially during the holidays. But the ham's the star—country ham, prosciutto, and a popular barbecued version known as "Preacher Ham." Last year the business shipped close to three thousand hams.

There's a fresh coat of white paint on the old building, an American flag next to the door, and red-and-white striped awnings. The sidewalk market in front is filled with carts that hold pansies and tomato plants in spring, fresh produce in summer, mums and pumpkins in fall. Inside, you can buy everything from old-fashioned coconut bonbons to laundry soap. There's homemade peanut brittle, cherry cobbler in a jar, spiced peaches, sorghum molasses, horehound candy, and vanilla chai latte.

There's no charge for the poetry, which Nancy writes. "Take some," reads a small sign next to stacks of loose sheets: "Thank you, Nancy."

There are two full-time employees—and they are like family. Lonnie Robinson has been working in the store for more than thirty years, Jessie Gray for fifteen. Jessie brings me a slice of prosciutto on waxed butcher paper; it was Jessie with whom I spoke a few years back when ordering a couple of hams for a niece's wedding in Miami. "That was you," he says, delighted. Most of those people down in Miami had never tasted a real country ham. It was gone in an hour. I knew after talking to Jessie that I had to get to Princeton.

 THOSE GUYS, THEY HAVE A LOVE FOR THIS BUSINESS," SAYS NANCY. "IT'S THEIR LIFE TOO. A COUPLE OF YEARS AGO, WE HAD SOME FREE-RANGE HAMS COME IN FROZEN. WE HAD TO WAIT TWO DAYS BEFORE I COULD PUT THEM IN SALT. MY FELLAS WERE NOT HAPPY. THEY TAKE PRIDE IN WHAT GOES ON WITH THOSE HAMS. IT COMES WITH THE HISTORY.

—Nancy Newsom

How many states does she ship to? "All of 'em. And England, Belgium, and Canada. Last Thanksgiving, we shipped one to a soldier in Afghanistan."

We hop into Nancy's red truck and drive two blocks to the ham house. The building has a heavy door and a huge padlock— it's a vault about the size of a large garage. It was built in 1963 by the Colonel in the backyard of the Cape Cod–style house where Nancy and her brother grew up, and where her ninety-three-year-old mother still lives today. "Daddy said he took an old process and put it in a new building," Nancy says, pushing open the door and ushering me inside.

It's dim, eerie, quiet—in fact, it reminds me of the feeling in the barrel warehouse of my grandfather's distillery, where there was a sign that read "Quiet, Bourbon Sleeping." The smell is deep and musty with a hint of smoke.

After the hams are delivered in January and February, they are rubbed with the brown sugar and salt mixture a few times, resting in between to absorb the rub. Then they are hand washed and taken to the ham house and hung on one of the thousands of nails driven into posts.

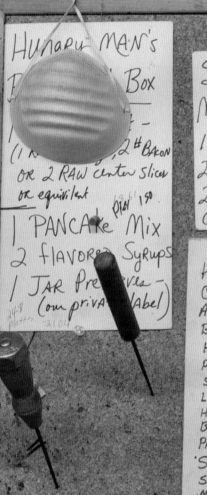

Hungry Man's
Breakfast Box
(1 #sausage, 2# Bacon
or 2 RAW center slices
or equivilent

1 PANCAKE Mix
2 flavored Syrups
1 JAR Preserves—
(our private label)

SMOKehouse
Meat Sampler

1 Roll Sausage
2# Sliced Bacon
2 RAW center slices
Co. Ham or equivilent, and
1/2 Pt. Sorghum Nuts-Candy

COUNTRY
Club
Co. Ham
Sandwich-8oz
Co Ham
Steak-11oz

Smoke 699 7301
HOFFman's Super Sharp 5.49
Colby   Julep—499   4.49
AMERICAN   4.99
Baby Swiss   4.99
HOT Pepper   3.49
Polish sausage   2.99
Souse Hot+mild   3.99
Liver Luf   4.49
Ham+cheese Loaf   4.99
Bolonga   2.29
Pickle+Pimintoloaf   4.29
Smoke Provolone   4.49
Smoke Gouda   5.99
Mozeralla   3.99
Smoked Gouda   5.49
Coby Jack   4.99
Bolo Hot   4.99
Trays-2.50 — Lg 3.00

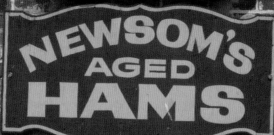

GARDEN SEED
AND PLANTS

THE OLD
MILL STORE

LAWN AND
GARDEN SUPPLIES

NEWSOM'S
AGED
HAMS

to
Historic
Princeton

"I burn green hickory in the big iron kettle," says Nancy, "and smoke them for weeks, off and on, depending on the weather. The smoke fills the whole room, and you can't see your hand in front of your face."

In time, a mold forms on the outside of each ham—just as each bourbon distillery has its own yeast, ham houses have their own mold, giving the ham its own distinct flavor, pungent and musty. During the aging process, the flesh of the ham expands into the outer covering of the mold in the heat of summer and contracts in winter, bringing with it the taste-enhancing enzyme—in the same way that Kentucky bourbon expands into the wood of its charred oak barrel and then contracts, pulling with it the oaky caramel flavor.

"We are the last to still do an ambient weather cure," Nancy says, "circulating the outdoor weather in and around our hams from the time they are out of salt in the springtime through the dog days of summer and into the fall, when they are finally ready to sell."

Newsom hams are anywhere from ten to twenty-two months old, and the older ones are neither hard nor dry. Why? Because the ham house that Bill Newsom built behind his house sits on low, swampy ground, where there's plenty of humidity. The hams are moist.

"Our forefathers," says Nancy, "developed this process because there was no refrigeration, and I feel that the preserving of this history has made us who we are today. I realized long ago that it was going to be a lost art."

In his book *Pig Perfect: Encounters with Remarkable Swine and Some Great Ways to Cook Them*, Peter Kaminsky, *New York Times* contributor, devotes an entire chapter— "The Ham Maker's Daughter"—to Nancy, whose hams "set the bar for America. In Spain, her hams would be a million-dollar business."

PETER KAMINSKY, *NEW YORK TIMES* CONTRIBUTOR, DEVOTES AN ENTIRE CHAPTER—"THE HAM MAKER'S DAUGHTER"—TO NANCY, WHOSE HAMS "SET THE BAR FOR AMERICA. IN SPAIN, HER HAMS WOULD BE A MILLION-DOLLAR BUSINESS."

She has been written about in *Gourmet, People, SlowFood USA, The New York Times* and the *Wall Street Journal*. She has spoken about the lost art of curing hams at the Southern Foodways Conference in Oxford, Mississippi, the International Food and Wine Expo at Disney World, and the national Fancy Food Show in New York. "I don't take my hams there, though," she says, "because I'm not in the wholesale business, and I don't want an order for so many hams that I can't fill it, because that's not my niche. It could be, but I don't want it to be.

"This business—the size of it—I have freedom. I can sleep at night. And it's going to stay that way. Sometimes I say to myself, 'What's wrong with you? You don't want this business to grow— if you don't grow, you'll die.' Well, that's not necessarily so."

Today, a Newsom ham hangs in a glass case in a museum in Aracena, a testament to the family legacy—and a reminder of the struggle to preserve it. I ask Nancy whether her twenty-nine-year-old son, John, who works part-time in the store, will choose to take up the task for the next generation. "Time will tell," she says. "He knows the process. He can do it all. If something happened to me tomorrow, John could do it."

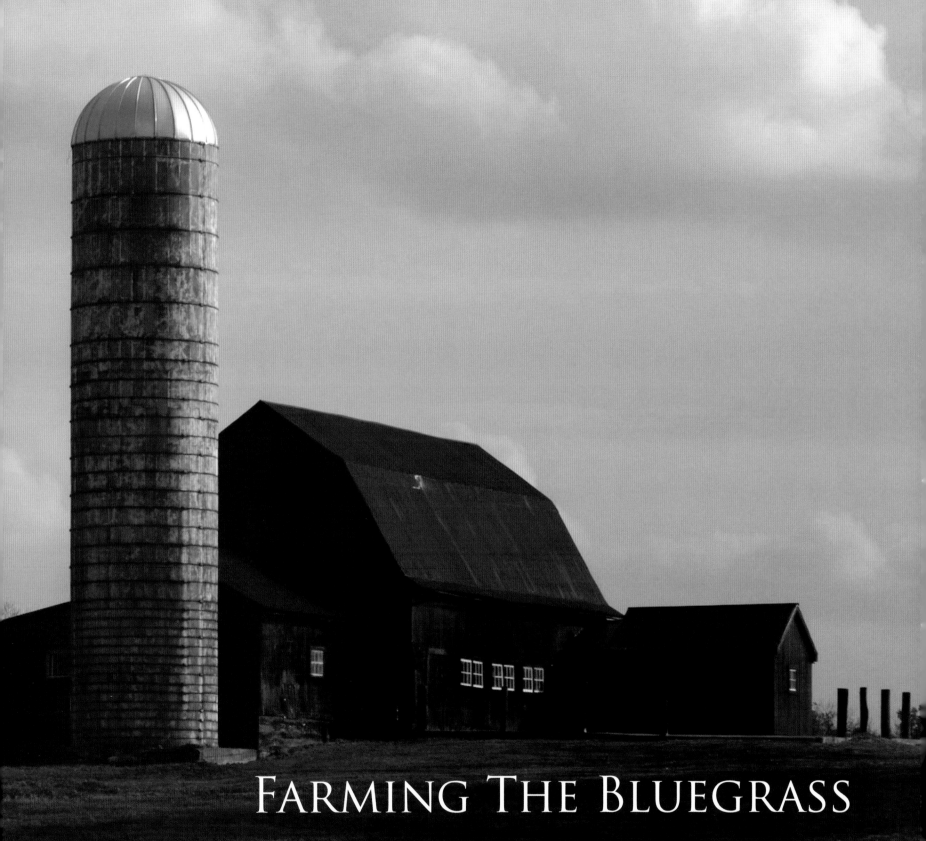

FARMING THE BLUEGRASS

When I was small, our eggs didn't come from the supermarket. My mom would stop at the Waters' farm, one hill over from our house, and buy a couple of dozen every week. In summer, there was a produce shack on River Road near the railroad tracks, and that's how I remember corn. Then, somewhere along the way, it became easier to just go to the A&P or Kroger, and we all forgot about finding farmers. They seemed to disappear down long dirt driveways somewhere in the country.

Today, with farmers' markets popping up all over, it looks as if small farms may be able to make a comeback after decades of decline. It looks as if there may be hope for farmers, once again, to make a decent living—farming.

Kentucky's agricultural roots are older than the state itself. Settlers who followed Daniel Boone into this part of the country brought seeds and livestock and cleared the land for farming. There was a time when Kentucky teemed with small farms—family farms that produced many things: hemp, vegetables, tobacco, wheat, sheep, hogs, cattle, horses. It was a good plan—a good way to live, economically, because if one crop failed there was always

a backup. Farmers knew how to raise a barn and kill hogs. They knew how to take their surplus tomatoes and beans and "put them up." Family farming meant children and parents working together, getting up early and doing chores, eating meals together, going to bed early. Neighbors helped neighbors. It was all part of farm culture. The community was centered on it.

After the Civil War, tobacco—especially the flavorful bright-leafed variety known as burley—became one of Kentucky's most profitable crops. During World War II, the War Department sent massive numbers of Lucky Strikes, Camels, and Chesterfields to soldiers overseas, and an entire generation came home addicted to cigarettes. The wars were good for the tobacco industry, and Kentucky was known for growing the finest in the world.

Both the plant and those who produced it were admired and respected, for the growing of burley was a great art. Even today, there are tobacco leaves all over the Kentucky State Capitol in Frankfort and the U.S. Capitol in Washington, D.C. Tobacco was more than just a crop. It was a symbol of America, a way of life.

" KENTUCKY IS UNIQUE FOR HAVING
SO MANY SMALL FARMS LEFT. THAT'S WHAT
TOBACCO DID FOR US. "

—Wendell Berry

In their beautiful book *Tobacco Harvest: an Elegy*, Wendell Berry and his friend the late photographer James Baker Hall captured a historical moment in 1973 in a Henry County tobacco patch—"a sort of interlude between the time when tobacco was an unquestioned, generally respected staple of our region's economy and the beginning of its precipitous decline both in reputation and in economic value." Berry describes harvesting a tobacco crop as "hard, hot, dirty, itchy, exhausting work, using up long days in August and September." The crew in the photographs "were friends and neighbors practicing the ancient custom of 'swapping work.' They were brought together by necessity and neighborliness, and also by friendship, old association, common history, and mutual respect…. They were responding to a recognized mutual need. They helped and they were helped, the relative amounts of work being far less important than the exchange itself."

I drove over to Henry County to see Wendell Berry and his wife, Tanya, on a blustery March day. Occupying a hill near the Kentucky River, the Berry farm is part of a landscape that has been home to the family for generations. Sheep graze on the slope next to the house, and the couple grow their own vegetables and produce much of the food they eat. We sat at the kitchen table, and I asked Wendell when he had started to worry about the path agriculture was taking.

He told me that when he and Tanya came back to Kentucky to live in 1964, the young people were leaving, and the spring lamb business, which had been a major agricultural industry here, was dying. "That different world that we went into at the end of World War II was forming itself with great speed.

"In 1952," he said, "Ezra Taft Benson—the man who said, 'Get big or get out'—had come in as secretary of agriculture, and the whittling away had begun. You could see that the integrity of the old agricultural communities was fading away." All over America, small family farms were disappearing and large commercial operations were taking over.

Then he explained about tobacco.

Until not very long ago, tobacco was a major cash crop in Kentucky, grown on a large number of small farms. Tobacco paid so well compared to other crops that a farmer could make a decent living without having to own or cultivate a lot of land. Many Kentucky tobacco farmers had jobs in town and grew tobacco on a few acres as well. Their day jobs may have paid most of the bills, but tobacco paid for extras—a new truck, college tuition for the kids. And because so many Kentuckians grew tobacco either part- or full-time, tobacco farmers were a powerful political force. For years, the U.S. government–administered tobacco program stabilized the price of tobacco and limited the amount that could be grown. That gave farmers a level of financial security that had been unheard-of in agriculture.

"Kentucky is unique for having so many small farms left," said Wendell. "That's what tobacco did for us." In the early seventies, tobacco farming was still pretty much intact, even though the 1964 surgeon general's report on smoking and health had increased the awareness of tobacco's risks. Not long after the report came out, filters were introduced, and darker, coarser tobacco replaced fine tobacco "up front." That took the emphasis off bright-leafed tobacco. Growers went from hand-ties to bales, and the art of tobacco farming began to diminish. Crop diversity began to disappear as well. "We tended away from a highly diversified farm economy and more and more in the direction of tobacco, because tobacco was the protected crop," Wendell explains. "If you have only one protected commodity on an agricultural market, then you are going to create a kind of gravitational force—more and more interest in that crop and less and less in everything else."

And that's what happened.

But even as Kentucky was becoming more dependent on tobacco, tobacco use was declining. Americans no longer wanted to give special protections to a crop that posed such serious health risks and costs, and in 2004 Congress ended the tobacco program. That, plus tobacco companies' increased use of cheap tobacco grown abroad, caused farmers' incomes to fall drastically. "And there we were," said Wendell, "with all these farmers who existed because they had been tobacco growers, and what were we going to do with them?"

Members of Congress from tobacco states were able to negotiate the Tobacco Transition Payment Program, also known as the tobacco buyout—money to help farmers transition from the guarantees and protections of the program. Four years earlier, state attorneys general had negotiated a national settlement with tobacco companies to reimburse states for some of the costs associated with smoking. Kentucky's share of the tobacco settlement was to be $1.7 billion over twenty-five years, and the state legislature decided the largest share of

that money should be appropriated to help farmers diversify—to help them build a new future.

Some farmers signed contracts with tobacco companies and started growing tobacco on an even larger scale than before. Some left farming altogether. But many looked for alternative crops—crops that would be as lucrative as tobacco, or at least close to it, and that could be grown on small acreage. With the help of buyout money—as well as grants from the tobacco settlement, ingenuity, creativity, and a lot of hard work—more and more farmers are finding ways. And at least some of the things that Wendell Berry has been talking about and writing about for years are beginning to happen.

Berry believes that if Kentucky agriculture is to be preserved, it will have to be preserved by Kentuckians. The answer, he believes, to surviving the global economy is local economy—people willing to get together and build a cooperative economy. "This is new ground, economically," he says. "People have got to understand that if we want a dependable food supply, we've got to cooperate to the extent of seeing that these farmers are paid enough to stay in the business."

Ask Wendell how we are doing so far and he answers, "We have begun. There weren't any farmers' markets a while ago. Now there are lots."

The U.S. Department of Agriculture says that in the last fifteen years, the number of farmers' markets across the country has jumped from 1,744 to 4,700, and Kentucky has mirrored that growth. And people are increasingly buying directly from local farmers through a program known as community supported agriculture (CSA), in which the consumer agrees to buy produce on a regular basis and pays the farmer in advance, thus sharing the risk of drought, disease, storms, and other disasters.

More and more of us are beginning to realize that the true cost of mass-produced cheap food is hidden. "It's a matter of common sense," says Wendell. "Our economy is dependent on the soil. We have to eat. The health of the land is all important."

A local economy, however, requires more people to work the land. Where we're going to find them is something that worries Wendell, for farming as a choice for young people is physically harder and economically riskier than most other lifestyles. Not

to mention heartbreak. "If you're a livestock farmer—if you have a breeding flock of ewes or cows or horses—you're going to experience your share of heartbreak. It's just going to happen. You're going to be looking at something that is beautifully made to live and it will be dead as a doornail. It happens over and over again. Crop failure, rains that come at the wrong time—you get tired. Probably," he says with a pause and a slow smile, "the best analogy is marriage. It's just the greatest thing in the world when you start out, but then you find you've got to work at it—and it involves days when you'd just as soon be someplace else."

According to the USDA 2007 census, Kentucky now has 85,000 small farms. "The question for all farms of limited acreage," says Wendell, "is how do you make that farm most productive and most sustainable within the given bounds. A thing that is limited can also be inexhaustible if the parts are properly put together and well husbanded."

Meet a few Kentuckians who are farming today with great eloquence.

greening the bluegrass

Leading to the front of the Bullitt family's ancestral home, Oxmoor, is a picturesque avenue of pin oaks planted by pioneer female landscape architect Marian Cruger Coffin in 1911.

Kay and Tommy Bullitt granted a preservation and conservation easement to the Commonwealth of Kentucky in 1991. Included were the ancestral home and outbuildings surrounded by 79.32 acres.

NEW LEASE ON LIFE

There are really two Oxmoors: The "mother" farm is a magnificent estate, home to five generations of the Bullitt family, its centerpiece a house begun in 1790. Then there are the forty-five acres of fertile fields that are separated from the mother farm by light-years and Interstate 64. This is Ivor's Oxmoor. At least fifteen acres of it.

The road to Ivor's first winds through a subdivision of pretty brick homes southeast of downtown Louisville, then bisects a golf course and passes in front of a country club. Then, just when you are sure you're lost, you come to a dirt road marked by a modest sign painted with colorful vegetables. It isn't the sort of approach you were expecting, but neither is Oxmoor a typical farm.

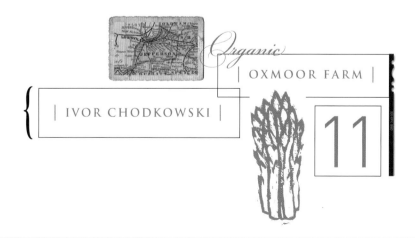

Organic

| OXMOOR FARM |

{ | IVOR CHODKOWSKI | }

11

Prominent attorney and one-time solicitor general, William Marshall Bullitt renovated the old frame and brick house, and after his marriage to Nora Iasigi, they retained architect F. Burrall Hoffman to enlarge it. The grandest private library in Kentucky was completed 1928.

Ivor Chodkowski stands in the middle of a brilliant field of kale. He's dressed in shorts and a T-shirt and wellies; a fresh-pulled beet is slung under his arm. He is talking on a cell phone, his facial features chiseled by both hardship and hope. Except for the phone, the beet, and the clothes, he might be Michelangelo's David, ready for anything.

Ivor is a full-time tenant farmer on fifteen acres of land at Oxmoor Farm. So many growing things: tomatoes, carrots, garlic, turnips, beans, chard, pumpkins, zinnias. The quiet is interrupted only by the downshift of a truck whizzing by on I-64 and the occasional smack of a golf ball when the wind is right.

THE LEASE THEY WORKED OUT GAVE NEW LIFE TO ONE OF LOUISVILLE'S OLDEST FARMS, A RURAL OASIS IN AN INCREASINGLY COMMERCIAL AND SUBURBAN AREA.

Ivor is in his fourteenth year of farming, his sixth here at Oxmoor. His family didn't farm but did spend summers in a rural area of New Hampshire, where young Ivor helped with chores at a neighboring farm—shoveling out the barn, feeding chickens, picking hay. "I tried some other things before I realized that was what I loved the most," he says.

Ivor's path intersected with Oxmoor Farm after an encounter with Nora Leake Cameron—or "Tooey," as she is called—who had made the trip from Washington, D.C., to visit her childhood home. Tooey and her sister, Nina, had grown up in the log house on the property during the fifties and sixties. Their grandparents, Nora and William Marshall Bullitt, lived in the big house called Oxmoor. The land on the far side of the interstate hadn't been used for years, and while looking things over, Tooey had an idea.

"I thought, why don't we have an organic garden out there?" she remembers. The next Saturday morning she drove to the farmers' market on Bardstown Road and began making inquiries. "That's when I met Ivor. He needed a place to farm." The lease they worked out gave new life to one of Louisville's oldest farms, a rural oasis in an increasingly commercial and suburban area.

When Ivor came to Oxmoor, he found a house, a barn, and a shed that hadn't been used for years and soil that had been untilled as far back as anybody could remember. The house was suitable for living quarters, and one of the first things he did was to start a program that would bring in three to four apprentice farmers per year in exchange for a stipend, housing, food from the farm, and workshops on farm-related topics: irrigation, soil, marketing, and so on.

One thing led to another. Not long after the apprenticeship program began, Tooey, Nina, and their cousins Porter and Lowry Watkins established the Shaw Scholarships. Named for William Shaw, Oxmoor's farm manager from 1929 to 1970, the program sponsors those who have been apprentices and want to become full-time organic farmers. "The Bullitts, in their generosity, help me pay those who are returning a more livable wage than I would be able to pay on my own," says Ivor.

"We all thought that this would be a good use of the land and a good way to give back," Tooey explains, her love for the old farm welling up. "There was all that land out there. It seemed right to connect it again with the rest of the world."

As a training site for new farmers, the suburban location has its advantages, says Ivor. "Because we're relatively close to town, it's never been difficult for us to find young people from town interested in farming—which is strange, because young people from rural areas are relatively uninterested, so there's something pretty wonderful going on. And the fact that apprentices have gone on to be farmers themselves is exciting. It relieves a worry of mine—that folks had no place to go after completing an apprenticeship. One of the biggest barriers has been land access. But as it turns out, there are lots of people who own land who aren't producers themselves and are willing to make that land available."

A FARMER WEARS MANY HATS— MARKETER, DISTRIBUTOR, PRODUCER— AND IT TAKES A UNIQUE PERSON TO PULL IT OFF.

"It's folks like me that are up to their ears in direct marketing," says Ivor. "We do multiple farmers' markets and Community Supported Agriculture (CSA). We're running around town dropping off to stores and restaurants, and we don't have the time we need to spend on the farm, producing. If I can make one delivery"—instead of several—"there's an enormous amount of time saved that I can spend back on the farm." In 2007, Ivor and three farmer partners started Grasshoppers, a local food distribution company. "It's unique," he says, "a multi-farm CSA operation that involves seventy farmers at the moment. After only two years we are looking at breaking even or maybe even making a small profit. What we do is facilitate the relationship between customer and producer."

The shares are for everything you can think of: produce, beef, lamb, chicken, eggs, goat cheese, cow cheese, farm-raised catfish, flowers, and the list goes on. "The CSAs are working really well. Now businesses are coming to us asking that we supply their employees—Brown-Forman, GE, E.ON. Last year there were eighty-five shares. This year there are four hundred."

As an entrepreneur who loves innovation, Ivor is now adding restaurateur to his collection of hats. The money for Harvest, a restaurant billed as the most local in town, has been raised in shares, and the goal is a menu that's 80 percent local. "It's one thing to have one or two items on the menu that are easily available and reasonably priced," says Ivor. "It's quite another thing entirely to construct a whole menu that's in season year-round and reasonably priced. February will be a challenge." And in keeping with his spread-the-wealth ethic, "We will train chefs to prepare local food and to go start their own restaurant. They'll spend time not only in the kitchen but on the farm as well."

CAROL GUNDERSON

Ivor also sits on the board of the Community Farm Alliance, a grassroots organization that "helps farmers help themselves." It's all part of his effort to make farming work and to take others along with him. Like his father, a University of Louisville professor for thirty-seven years, Ivor is a born teacher, and thus the old farm has become an incubator for new ideas and a new generation of farmers, teaching them both old and new ways and sending them out into Kentucky with an alternate vision: You don't have to go corporate. None of this would be possible on this fifteen-acre field of dreams—no kale, no yellow buses, no Shaw Scholars— were it not for Oxmoor Farm and the Bullitt family who, through the scholarship program, are spreading the message of organic farming all over the state.

Organic

| OXMOOR FARM |

{ | THE FOOD LITERACY PROJECT AT OXMOOR | }

In 2004, a local teacher asked Ivor Chodkowski if she could bring her students to Oxmoor Farm for a hands-on experience. Realizing the visit was more than he could handle, the busy farmer nevertheless recognized a tremendous opportunity.

So, with the help of Carol Gunderson, who has a background in food- and farm-based environmental education, he started Oxmoor Farm's apprenticeship program. Two years later they began the Food Literacy Project, a nonprofit educational agency that brings urban communities in Louisville back to the roots of their food.

> **THE GOAL IS TO ENHANCE THE KNOWLEDGE AND SKILLS NEEDED TO MAKE FOOD CHOICES THAT ARE HEALTHY FOR PEOPLE, THE ENVIRONMENT, AND THE LOCAL COMMUNITY,"** SAYS CAROL. **"STUDENTS ARE EMPOWERED TO TAKE HEALTHY EATING INTO THEIR OWN HANDS BY GROWING AND PREPARING THEIR OWN FOOD.**

"Carol has taken full advantage of the farm and is using it to educate future generations as to where their food comes from," says Ivor. "It's a happy coincidence that this farm is in town and available—and easily accessible. It's much less likely that this program would happen if the farm were even an hour from town."

In 2009, according to Carol, 87 percent of the students visiting the farm qualified for free or reduced-price lunches at school. Many live in neighborhoods described as food deserts, meaning that their families have limited access to fresh produce and are overexposed to fast food. "The experience of making homemade bread, harvesting vegetables, and developing their own recipes," says Carol, "deepens students' understanding about where food comes from, how it grows, and how it can be used to nourish their bodies in healthy ways."

Children come by the bus load, spilling onto the soil of a real working farm to pop carrots out of the ground, hold wriggling earthworms, and munch vegetable tacos. It's an eye-opening experience, judging from their comments: "It smells like nature out here." "Gimme some more spinach." "I didn't know that so much food comes from a farm."

"Ivor was a huge part of the vision for this project. He was willing to let kids tramp through his fields and taste things."

And clearly he's thinking in line with others. Michelle Obama, as first lady, started a vegetable garden at the White House. Then in February 2010 she made childhood obesity her signature issue. This is more evidence that initiatives like the Food Literacy Project at Oxmoor Farm are part of a national trend toward healthier eating.

BEST-LAID PLANS

Jon Brumley says he's odd man out around Shelby County because he's not raising tobacco or running cattle. "They refer to us as alternative farmers, which sounds like we're raising dope. But I'm farming like my great-grandfather did. My father, my grandfather, my great-grandfather, they had multiple sources of income on this farm, and that's the way it's gotta be. Back then you had to have two or three income sources, and everything had to articulate and work together. That's what people are going to have to learn to do again in order for small farming to come back. Because when one is down, another will be up."

Over the past thirteen years, Jon and his wife, Norma, have done everything from growing vegetables to killing chickens. "We've done it all," says Jon, "and now we're peddling eggs. We've found a niche. But the other farmers, they look at us as kind of odd."

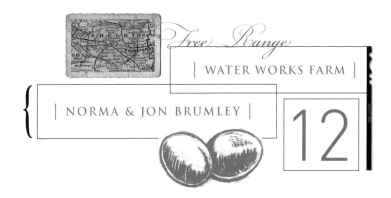

Free Range

| WATER WORKS FARM |

{ | NORMA & JON BRUMLEY | }

12

Jon grew up milking cows and raising tobacco on the farm that his great-grandfather bought in 1923. "This would have been considered a thirty-cow farm," says the jovial Jon, who has big, round, baby-blue eyes that make him look younger than his forty-seven years. "Up until about 1970, there were tons of these little farms that would support twenty to thirty dairy cows, a couple of sows and a hog, raise four or five acres of tobacco—enough to feed and support a family at that time."

After joining the Air Force and learning aviation mechanics, Jon met and married Norma Ritter. The couple lived in Hazard, where they operated a small but successful aviation business in the Eastern Kentucky mountains.

Norma had grown up on a farm as well, and as a child, she was the one who went to the henhouse to collect eggs. "For some reason, my brothers and sisters were never around. So I guess I've been farming all my life," says Norma. "I guess it's just who I am."

In 1997, the couple decided to come back to the family farm to be near Jon's parents and "to do whatever it took to make a living. I'm the last of thirteen," says Norma. "I can handle anything." Nonetheless, the first time she saw the clump of woods that was to become Water Works Farm, she cried.

"Jon said, 'Norma, can't you see it?' I couldn't see it."

Since then they've scratched out a living growing vegetables and hay, raising tobacco and free-range chickens. "We've done it all," says Norma. "We've just had to change it up, try different things, see what worked. We tinkered around out in the yard, put some five-gallon buckets on pallets—next thing you know, we've got a double-bay greenhouse out there and something like six hundred tomato plants. We've just ventured into so many different things, and we've taught ourselves, either by just doing it or through reading various books." The county extension office "has been very helpful to small farmers as they've diversified away from tobacco," she adds. "They are truly a large source of information."

For years, Norma and Jon made the thirty-mile trip into Louisville each Saturday morning to sell their hydroponic tomatoes, chicken, and a few dozen eggs at the Bardstown Road Farmers' Market. The chicken, which they mainly sold to high-end grocery stores and restaurants, was a mammoth amount of work, "but the Saturday morning market was a reward," says Norma. "I loved my customers. I told them, if something isn't right, you let us know about it and we'll make it right."

It's very difficult for small farmers to pay help, and while there's profit in the meat business, there's not as much as you might think. "It's very similar to dairy farming. You are required to be here all the time," says Norma. "Jon and I took a vacation three years ago. First time in twenty years. So two years ago we dropped the meat birds and decided to go strictly to eggs. Profitwise, it's unbelievable. Laborwise, it's a whole lot easier. Yes, yes, yes."

CANDLING THE EGGS

In keeping with their philosophy of multiple income sources, the Brumleys contracted with five other farmers around the state, initially supplying them with chickens that would be raised with all-natural feed—no chemicals, no hormones, and no antibiotics. Each farmer agreed to supply a certain number of eggs per week—which they would deliver to Water Works Farm twice weekly. Jon would deliver from there. The flocks would be staggered as far as laying cycle, keeping a year-round supply of eggs.

"I hustled eggs like nobody's business," Jon says. "You gotta be mobile, agile, and hostile. It's all about customer service and continuity."

Former dairy farmers, according to Jon, make the best chicken farmers. The chickens are raised in the old dairy barn and turned out to pasture every day. Jon turns his chickens out in the huge bright green alfalfa field out back. They pretty much have the run of the place, but "most of the time they spend laying in the shade dusting themselves." The donkeys? "That's protection from the coyotes."

After the eggs are dropped off, they're cleaned. Before Norma got her commercial egg washer, she would take the eggs into the kitchen of the farmhouse and wash them one by one. Hundreds of them. Now there's a brand-new egg washer in the former greenhouse. "We call this room the eggplant," says Jon, never without his sense of humor. "Gonna paint the top green and the bottom purple."

Jon has a big heart and always has time to share his knowledge with other farmers, and word has it that anyone who comes into the extension office with an entrepreneurial idea is sent to Jon. "There's no sense in them having to reinvent the wheel."

How's business?

"Real good," says Jon. "When I started out, I was putting twelve cases in my truck. Now I'm putting sixty." That's ten thousand to twelve thousand eggs a week that Jon wholesales, under the label Shelby Pride, to venues such as Whole Foods, Good Food Co-Op, Creation Gardens, 211 Clover Lane, Rainbow Blossom Natural Food Markets, and so on.

"Now we're going to start supplying Corbett's with quail eggs. Yep, a blind squirrel finds a nut once in a while," he says with a big smile. Jon used to have a saying: "If you want a watermelon, ask for a big doggone watermelon. Don't ask for a little one, 'cause you're gonna come away hungry."

Today, Jon Brumley is a happy man, his domain six acres of hallowed ground tucked into the hundred-acre family farm. It includes 2,500 Hy-Line Brown chickens, a little tobacco, and three donkeys for protection from the coyotes. "I hate to say it, but I'm kind of living my dream right now. It's fun. I drive an old car, I drive an old truck, I like being at Whole Foods, I like having my ego stroked."

That watermelon?

"Maybe I learned I didn't need it. Nope, I think I'm past that."

QUAIL EGGS

JARED AND KENNY MATTINGLY

SAY CHEESE!

Years ago, a high school sociology teacher told a friend of mine, "You want to be a farmer? That's for people who can't do anything." Those days are gone, and good riddance. (That friend, by the way, has now been farming for twenty years.) Today, people are more appreciative of the complexity of the work. Successful farmers have always been those rare individuals who can balance a respect for tradition with the willingness to innovate.

Meet Ken Mattingly. Kenny makes cheese.

Dairy

| KENNY'S FARMHOUSE CHEESE |

| THE MATTINGLY FAMILY |

13

Pl. Asiago
09-10-13   15/10

Pl. Asiago
09-10-13   15-22

Cumin Seed Gouda
10-1-09

Cumin Seed Gouda
10-1-09

Sm. Gouda 9/23 14.68

Sm. Gouda 9/23 14.10

Cumin Seed Gouda
10-1-09

Sm Gouda
10-9-09

Sm. Gouda
10·9·09

Sm·Gouda 9/23

Sm·Gouda 9/23·14·8

Sm Gouda 9/23

Sm Gouda 9/23 13·24

09·10·13
P.C. Asiago

09·10·13 15 – 4
P.C. Asiago

In the early 1990s, as a young dairy farmer, Ken accepted an invitation to attend the International Trade Conference in Brussels. At the time, his family was struggling to make a living with seventy cows and two hundred acres in Barren County. While abroad, Ken visited different types of farms. In Eastern Europe, he saw huge operations: dairies that milked four thousand cows and pig farms with eight hundred sows. In Western Europe, on the other hand, he found the owners of small farms adding value to their products, marketing them locally, and even setting their own prices. He was especially impressed with a young husband and wife in Holland who were making Gouda cheese on their thirty-cow farm. "They weren't rich, but they were doing just fine," he says. "That model of agriculture got in my head, and I came home with a new vision."

In 1998, after much research, Kenny and his wife, Beverly, bought some used equipment and, with the old-world techniques he had learned in Holland, began using some of their farm's milk to produce Gouda cheese. That first year they made four thousand pounds of it. Last year the Mattinglys produced seventy thousand pounds of cheddar, Colby, Asiago, Jack, Swiss, Havarti, and some superb blues.

The rolling pastureland of south-central Kentucky looks a lot like the farmland of Western Europe. Pretty country, it's not far from Mammoth Cave National Park. Up until the seventies, the state of Kentucky was the second biggest milk producer in the country, and Barren County was rife with small family farms that raised dairy cattle and tobacco. But in the years that followed, as the trend became "Get big or get out," many families sold out to bigger interests; nowadays a single farm might support up to as many as a thousand beef cattle. "These kinds of operations are just destroying the farms," says Kenny. "That's what some people think they have to do to survive. But I looked at that scene. I don't want to get big. So this is the alternative."

This morning, in the spotless cheese-making room, Kenny is making one of the newer cheeses, a Gruyère style called Norwood. The work begins at 4 A.M. with milk fresh from the cow. "The temperature of the milk as it comes from the cow is ideal for cheese making," Kenny says. "We don't cool it or anything. It just comes from the cow—next door, through that pipe, and right into this vat. To me, that complements our cheese: the freshness, the low carbon footprint."

Kenny stirs the raw milk constantly, heating it and adding a bacterial culture from France that naturally begins the conversion to cheese. "There are only two cheeses that we make that are cooked above the cow's body temperature," he explains as he begins draining the whey from the stainless steel vat: "Norwood and Asiago." Because the milk is so fresh, pasteurizing is not necessary.

Lined up on shelves, ready for the cooler, are beautiful chunks of pale golden cheese—white cheddar, the Mattinglys' best seller. Newly made, it looks like Carrara marble and smells like fresh bread. Each block weighs forty pounds.

Beverly Mattingly handles the packing and shipping, along with two dedicated employees. Every step—cutting, waxing, wrapping, labeling, and packing—is done by hand. "There are things that could be done to speed the process," Beverly admits. "Brushing the wax onto the wheels is time-consuming, but of course, that's what makes it so special."

The Mattinglys' twenty-two-year-old son manages the farm. Now in his last year of business school, Jared Mattingly is on the farm every weekend. He also spends a couple of days there during the week, to give the farmhands some time off. "He's not real involved in the cheese business right now," says his dad. "Down the road, I think he will be. He handles all of this real well for a twenty-two-year-old. That's where half my enthusiasm comes from to keep on—the fact that he's interested."

The 120 or so cows are mostly Holsteins, "but we've been crossbreeding to European breeds," Ken says, "like Jersey and Swedish Red and Montbeliarde, which are primarily used in the French Alps, because we want an animal that's more willing to graze on grass; it produces a richer milk, a richer cheese." The cows are raised without synthetic hormones and supplement their pasture diet with homegrown forage and purchased grain. The goal is to get them on pasture as much as possible. "Grass is the best environment," says Ken, "and it makes financial sense. They do their own harvesting, they're healthier, and they spread their own manure when they're out there."

The Mattinglys practice what they call biological farming. "We pay close attention to the biology of the soil," says Ken. "Organic matter, mineralization. We backed away from being certified organic. There's a huge learning curve, a huge amount of paperwork, and it's very expensive. I want to produce our cheese in a way that's good for the consumer and good for us. If I'd continued to try to be organic I wouldn't be in business, because I couldn't learn it fast enough and grow this business. It was costing me too much to produce feed. I buy grain now for three hundred dollars a ton; organic feed is a thousand dollars. So I guess it's all about sustainability and balancing things."

Today the Mattinglys age thirty types of cheese in their cooler, and their market has expanded to stores in ten states. They also sell through farmers' markets and via the Internet.

So, what's the big picture for small farms in Kentucky from where Kenny stands?

"The reality is, the majority of our vegetables are still coming from Florida and California. I'm thankful for our customers; our business has grown. But there are people who talk about how important local food is and yet you can't sell them anything—it all comes down to the bottom line. They can get it cheaper off a truck somewhere. That's part of it.

MARY ROSE AND JARED

"The other part is, there is opportunity, but the majority of farmers are not taking advantage of it. There's a bigger demand for farm products than farmers are producing. For those who are willing to get out of their comfort zone, there is opportunity, because there has been a change in the culture. Consumers are looking at what small farmers can produce and how they're producing it. So there's a gap that needs to be bridged, and some of the work needs to be done by the consumer and some of it by the farmer.

"I think farmers try to fool you sometimes, especially young farmers. They think they've got it all figured out—driving a big diesel truck, got some cows in the field, living on their dad's or their grandfather's hard work. So I think we've got to make changes in how we do things in order to preserve what's really important.

"I've never been one to think I've got it figured out. I've been making Kentucky Blue for five years. It's an outstanding cheese. But every day I'm thinking, 'How can I make it better?'"

> " ONE FARM IN OHIO, WE GAVE OUR GOUDA RECIPE. THEY HAD THE NUMBER ONE IN THE COUNTRY FOUR YEARS AGO. I FELT I NEEDED TO PASS ON WHAT THOSE EUROPEAN FARMERS HAD PASSED ON TO ME. THEY OPENED THEIR DOOR... "
>
> —Ken Mattingly

Like so many of the farmers I spoke with, Ken is paying it forward, helping other farmers get started in the cheese business. "They've read about us and come over here to get our recipes," he says.

"You gave them your recipes?" I ask.

"One farm in Ohio, we gave our Gouda recipe. They had the number one in the country four years ago. I felt I needed to pass on what those European farmers had passed on to me. They opened their door…"

As someone who uses every bit of his ingenuity to make his farm sustainable, Ken encourages other farmers to think out of the box. "I tell them instead of getting bigger, they can be successful by adding value to their product. I've done it. Others can do it too. There are lots of other methods that can be applied."

Some operations don't care about the next generation.
It doesn't matter as long as they've made their money.
I want to farm in a way that gives my son out there
a future. I want these fields to produce for
him better than they are for me.

—Ken Mattingly

ACKNOWL

When I finished *But Always Fine Bourbon*, I thought that I would never write another book. That lasted about two weeks.

Books come from a passion and this one would never have been written were it not for the passion of those who told me their stories, who allowed me into their lives. And it would never have come to fruition without the passion of our "dream team," who together produced the beautiful work you see before you: photographer Thom Shelby who, with his easy-going sense of humor and ability to capture the soul, was a joy to work with. The effervescent and multi-talented Mary Dennis Kannapell, whose positive attitude and ability to take any task in a zillion creative directions is responsible for the design, along with Elizabeth Perry Spalding, who spent two months in front of her computer getting it right – turning pictures and prose into this rich work. My editors, Sara Tucker, Jill Keeney and Jim Oppel, whose advice and support were both extraordinary and indispensable. They made me think – and kept my voice. And Nancy Heinonen, our Production Manager, for her enthusiasm, her guidance and most of all for her business sense. All of these people gave of themselves because of their love for this project – with little thought of return.

My love and thanks to my husband, Tinsley, for once again putting up with all of this with typical grace and good humor – and for keeping things running on the home front. And to my wonderful and ever-encouraging sons and daughters-in-law, Ward and Chamie and Van and Ashley, who read and inspired – and were easy on Mom.

It's hard to know what to say to Christy and Owsley Brown who have nurtured so much that is Kentucky. Simply put, they were here for us from beginning to end. A huge thank you as well to the green, green, Gill Holland whose input, advice and support have been invaluable.

EDGMENTS

Special thanks to Tanya and Wendell Berry for so patiently and thoughtfully leading me through tobacco history – and the future of small farms – an important part of this story. And for encouraging me to remove my rose-colored glasses.

I am especially grateful for the dear friends who read, critiqued, advised and cheered me on, especially Bebe Bleakley, Rae Horton, Dr. Sam Thomas, Mary Oppel, Marchant Reutlinger, Sue Todd, Mary Donald and as always, Kitty and Monk Terry and Sissy and Julian Van Winkle.

I would also like to thank David Morgan, Meme Runyon and River Fields, William Morrow, Dale Fisher, Buzz Carloftis, Jane Hardy, Sharon Corcione, Valencia Libby, Margaret Clay, Madison Culler, Judi Jennings, Aloma Dew, Haviland Argo, Toss Chandler, Lawrence Jelsma, Carl Pollard, Alex Gans, Jim Couch, Martha Neal Cooke, George Gatewood, Bill Combs, Betsy Johnston, Andrea Kannapell, Cheryl and "Cap" Middleton, and Scott and Stokes A. Baird in Munfordville, Jenny Wigginton and Donna Cornell in Bloomfield, Teri Blanton, Jerry Hardt, Kevin Pentz and Burt Lauderdale in eastern Kentucky, Michael Aldridge, George Dick, and especially Blair Shelby for putting up with her exquisitely talented Thom.

There were many more stories we wanted to tell, especially those of Sallie Bingham and the Wolf Pen Branch Mill Farm, the Henry Wallace family, Joan and John Mayer and their family over at Nursery Place, Bob Horton and Bob Gatewood of Longwood Antique Wood, and Bill Weyland, who is helping to give historic buildings in downtown Louisville a new lease on life. We ran out of time – but next time. Thank you all.

TREEHOUSE,
WOODLAND
FARM

ROUND BARN, MUNFORDVILLE
STOKES A. & MARY SCOTT BAIRD
Design by Scott Tichenor and Jim Hatfield

Kentucky

THE OHIO RIVER